Late Hirschman

Albert Hirschman's Legacy
Works and Discussions

Luca Meldolesi
Series Editor

Vol. 5

Luca Meldolesi

Late Hirschman

Theoretical exercises in "self-subversion"

PETER LANG

New York - Berlin - Bruxelles - Chennai - Lausanne - Oxford

Library of Congress Cataloging-in-Publication Control Number: 2023039249

Bibliographic information published by the Deutsche Nationalbibliothek.
The German National Library lists this publication in the German
National Bibliography; detailed bibliographic data is available
on the Internet at http://dnb.d-nb.de.

Cover design by Peter Lang Group AG

ISSN 2576-9723 (print)
ISBN 9781636675404 (hardback)
ISBN 9781636675510 (ebook)
ISBN 9781636675527 (epub)
DOI 10.3726/b21041

Published by Peter Lang Publishing Inc., New York, USA
info@peterlang.com - www.peterlang.com

This publication has been peer reviewed.

CONTENTS

PREFACE

> "It is absolutely necessary for Europe to continue on its path toward greater unity and keep Germany on board (*addossée*). What is regrettable is that a sufficiently strong cultural feeling has not developed among the citizens of Europe. Too much emphasis has been placed on the economic aspect, thinking that the rest would come by itself." "Do you agree [then] with Robert Schuman's declaration," asks the interviewer, "that 'if we could start over I would begin with culture?'" "Yes, absolutely."
>
> Albert Hirschman
>
> "*Evenement du jeudi*," May 25, 1995[1]

(1) Begun as a simple intellectual exercise, the present work has picked up along the way some additional reasons to justify the "wear and tear" involved in its construction. Perhaps initially a certain weight was given to the aspiration to keep alive a Colornian-Hirschmanian work experience of many years duration. Then the wish took over to (once again) honor Albert Hirschman, now deceased—the desire to avoid losing the many small memories that bind me to him, to better understand his views, to (possibly) make progress on some of the vexed questions that had "intrigued" me in the past—and also to break

1 "If I have one quality," he adds further on (cf. box 72, folder 13), "it is that I try and master the things that attract my attention and then to make them my own. The free man is one who goes out to meet the unexpected and constantly strives to question himself."

away, in this regard, from any sort of ritualism. Albert did not like "orthodoxies." At a conference in his honor in Buenos Aires in 1989 he said this explicitly.[2] Nevertheless, since his departure some different (and conflicting) ways of encapsulating (and perhaps "canonizing") his work have emerged, from which it is well to shy away.[3]

As a reasonable alternative, partial as it may be, it seems to me possible to turn to the careful exploration of an example. We can in fact embark on the in-depth reconstruction of some specific themes that show the richness and importance of his cognitive contribution (undertaken from my own approach, inevitably[4]—that of "an Italian" as Albert used to call me, with a hint of irony, superiority and maybe even envy—he the German-American, of course, but "without a country"). And which consequently give a genuine idea, *urbi et orbi*, of what and how much can be learned from him by normally educated people from different social science disciplines (who are of course sufficiently motivated and willing to make the effort).

In other words, through small ad hoc exercises in "triggering" the cultural and political potential of Albert's work, it is possible, in my view, to combat current attempts to "homogenize" his unmistakable point of view. For it is indeed one which, springing from the insights of Eugenio Colorni and from his own youthful experiences, the author invented and diligently pursued throughout his life. It is this that we must take in and apply (in the most diverse fields and situations), and also, to the best of our ability, creatively and innovatively repurpose—so that we can continue the journey.

2 Cf. Hirschman (1995, p. 69); and ch. 1, n. 20 below.

3 Without naming any names, I refer here to certain recurring "sins"—such as "dicing," for example—cutting Hirschman's work into "slices" according to discipline, or alternatively, "summarizing." It is clear, in fact, that since the sad juncture of our author's passing, numerous intellectuals have thought to simply recall an aspect of Hirschman's work that appealed to them. Others have instead succumbed to the temptation to "capture" the part of his work that fits with their own discipline (economics, political science, culture history, etc.), while still others have published questionable summaries of Albert's contribution—improvisations that certainly do not do him justice.

4 Obviously, the subjective aspect of the analysis can never be completely suppressed—as Colorni had taught Hirschman. The idea is rather to keep that aspect consciously "in check," to allow a (relatively) *more* objective analysis. And furthermore, I would like to clarify that it is possible to disarmingly acknowledge the (spatio-temporal, personal) angle that such an analysis comes from, not least in order to construct the argument more explicitly—as, in fact, we will try to do in the following pages.

(2) Before moving forward it is important that we establish a starting point. It is well-known that after the success of *Exit, Voice, and Loyalty* (1970), Hirschman increasingly followed the interdisciplinary (or trans-disciplinary) leanings that he later called "trespassing," and mapped out *The Passions and the Interests* (written essentially in 1972–1973, a sabbatical year at the Institute for Advanced Study). Moreover, he gave up his teaching position at Harvard[5] and moved to the Institute at Princeton, where he was asked to set up the School of Social Science together with Clifford Geertz, the great American anthropologist, with whom he became friends.[6] Together with Bill Sewell and Quintin Skinner, Hirschman and Geertz then wrote, in 1977, a brief programmatic text that we can take as the "overture" to our line of thinking.[7]

It concerns the proposal, put forward together with the Institute's School of Historical Studies, of a three-year program of study on "the ways in which a society's perception or analysis of itself influences the responses of that society to the challenges or problems which confront it. While much work has been done," the text continues, "on the perception which societies have of themselves, and also on social or political action pursued in response to perceived challenges, much less attention has been devoted to the way in which the perception or the self-analysis helps to define those challenges and the responses to them. It is this interplay between self-interpretation and action, as a generating force in history, which seems to us to deserve special study as part of a collaborative enterprise between historians and social scientists."[8]

5 Not only because he had lost interest in teaching, he told me, but because maintaining Harvard's teaching standards required constantly keeping up to date in economics (international, development, Latin American, etc.), which did not fit with his research priorities. But as we shall soon see, the real reason goes deeper (cf., also, ch. 2, n. 93).

6 Concerning their meeting and the intellectual partnership between Hirschman and Geertz, see Adelman (2013, p. 500).

7 The first of the two texts, *Self-Perception, Mutual Perception, and Historical Development* (School of Social Science, 1977), was (in part) for a grant application to the "National Endowment for the Humanities," which was later awarded. On the other hand, according to Wolf Lepenies' testimony, the formation of the group of intellectuals who were to develop the program ran into a number of practical difficulties. These problems were repeated later when Geertz and Hirschman, now retired, persuaded certain intellectuals to move to the Institute in their place. Thus, despite the contributions of Michael Walzer and Joan Scott, it can be said that, throughout its early phase, the Institute's School of Social Science lived primarily on the truly extraordinary personal efforts of the two founders.

8 School of Social Science (1977, p. 1). "Apart from its considerable intrinsic interest," the text continues, "such an enterprise would indeed help to break down interdisciplinary

The text then offers a fascinating exemplification of various areas of research on which such a collaborative effort might concentrate—such as decline, underdevelopment and "loss," success and defeat, revolution, a review of the idea of "influence," along with East-West and North-South mutual perceptions. And it indicates that "the scholars concerned would be drawn from a wide range of disciplines—anthropology, political, social and cultural history including the history of art, political science, and economics."

There is in addition a second text, a simple note, perhaps contemporary, in which Sewell, Skinner, Geertz and Hirschman clarify the position of the nascent School of Social Science.[9] "We do not normally attempt to engage in large-scale statistical or quantitative analysis [. . .] nor do we see ourselves primarily as problem-solvers working to come up with prescriptions for the current ills of society (although some of our members have had active interests in policy questions)" [including Hirschman, of course]. "The main focus of our attention is more interpretative: we are mainly concerned, as we have always been, with investigating the meanings of social behavior and the determinants of social change, and continue to be resolutely multi-disciplinary, comparative and international in our approach."[10]

Now, if we read these programmatic passages retrospectively, in light of the scientific output from Albert that followed, we realize that they accentuate a significant aspect of his overall work. What they do, in fact, relative at least to Hirschman's inevitably scientific early training (i.e., oriented toward economics, mathematics, and statistics), *sui generis* as it was, and to his well-known

barriers both between history and social science, and among the various branches of history on the one hand and of social science on the other."

9 School of Social Science (1977a).

10 School of Social Science (1977a, p. 7). "We strive to base our work on historical as well as contemporary problems, and on ethnographic as well as quantitative findings. We are, moreover, concerned with the use of such empirical data to criticize and refine the prevailing theories and methodologies of the human sciences. [. . .] While the long-dominant approach in social science has some real achievements to its credit, we share many of the reservations increasingly being expressed about it: namely, that its methods and procedures have resulted in over-specialization, present-mindedness and unwarranted scientism without much compensating capacity to provide satisfactory solutions to the pressing social and economic problems of the day. Even if we were happier with the achievements of American social science, we would still insist that the range of techniques it characteristically employs have prevented a number of important questions about the social world from even being asked. To put the matter at its simplest, we feel that there has been a tendency to focus exclusively on questions of social causation at the expense of studying social meanings."

"trilogy" on development and Latin America,[11] and also relative to *Exit*, is make more explicit an *intellectual re-balancing* on Albert's part in the direction of the "humanities."[12]

In addition, as we know, his first collection of Princeton essays—*Essays in Trespassing. Economics to Politics and Beyond* (1981)—organizes the texts "around" five monographs,[13] as if to underscore (and accentuate) the "multi-disciplinary, comparative and international" aspects that indeed pervade his entire oeuvre. And again, in all probability *Shifting Involvements* (1982), at least in its initial inspiration, had the aim of responding to the dictates of this new phase.[14] And even the texts of retrospective reflection, written for *The New Palgrave, a Dictionary of Economic Theory and Doctrine* (1987) and published in *Rival Views of Market Society* (1986), are undoubtedly essays by the Princeton Hirschman.

It just so happened, incidentally, that Nicoletta Stame and I got to know Albert precisely during this evolutionary period and then followed him step by step in his ongoing journey—which involved the need to curb the ultra-liberal [ultra-free-market] thinking then triumphant on the wings of the Reagan presidency (and would lead Albert, in the mid-1980s, down the path to *The*

11 Referring, of course, to *The Strategy of Economic Development* (1958), *Journeys Toward Progress* (1963) and *Development Projects Observed* (1967).

12 "While quantitative research has obviously an important role to play," we indeed read further along in School of Social Science (1977a, p. 8), "we believe that the significance of most quantitative findings cannot be properly analyzed or appreciated outside the context of social meanings. This implies that, rather than confining ourselves exclusively to statistical and mathematical methods borrowed from the natural sciences, we must also employ humanistic approaches borrowed from such fields as linguistics, history, literary criticism and philosophy. These observations have particular force, we feel, in the study of social change, which is the principal focus of our School." Later, in a letter to Paul Krugman dated January 10, 1994 (box 54, folder 4), Albert would argue that languages, metaphors, myths, stories are other useful ways of knowing that should not be neglected.

13 "The arrangement," Hirschman (1981, pp. v–vi) explains in the Preface to the volume, "makes plain that my interests have moved away from the exclusive concerns with development issues [. . .]. First place has been given to the essay "The Rise and Decline of Development Economics," in part because it helps explain this shift. It is not so much that the decline made me move on to greener pastures; rather, I came to feel that progress with some of the major puzzles in economic-political development requires considerable detours and forays into other areas."

14 Cf., below, ch. 3. Even *Getting Ahead Collectively* (1984a), which takes up some of the themes of *The Strategy*, contributes significantly to this issue, especially through the "principle of conservation and mutation of social energy."

Rhetoric, 1991). This was the long season of honorary degrees and the translations of his work into many languages, European and Asian (which would significantly increase his overall cultural influence)—the season of reflection that followed the fall of the Berlin Wall and would contribute to the suggestion of a new "fine-tuning" of his work.

It is these stages, still fresh in the memory of the present writer, that provide the backdrop for the pages that follow, and which make it possible to clarify, at least in part, the meaning of "late" Hirschman's "re-entry" into German culture and politics.[15] Beyond the obvious cultural and human significance of this re-entry after such an extended period—one is tempted to ask whether Albert's new work mainly from within a unifying Germany also represented, at least in his implicit intentions, a way of contributing indirectly to the emergence of a new feeling and a new European culture in the making.

Look again at the epigraph that opens this preface. Actually, to someone like the writer, who knew and worked with Albert during that period, it seems a plausible hypothesis that according to the rationale of self-subversion he would have wished in a certain sense to "reposition himself," not least mentally, between Princeton and Berlin in order to be able to move more nimbly on both chessboards—with a view of ultimately re-introducing, as regards Europe, his entire body of work as a contribution to initial efforts to bridge (at least in part) the deficit in European construction which, in the mid-1990s of the last century, he had so explicitly noted.[16]

(3) Thanks to the exceptional nature of the story it tells and the theoretical distinctions Hirschman drew from it, the exploration undertaken in the now-famous essay that opens *A Propensity to Self-Subversion* (1995)—"Exit, Voice, and the Fate of the German Democratic Republic"—lends itself surprisingly well to introducing the point of the present paper. That is to say, it makes the very useful suggestion that by rereading certain texts and making

15 "Having been away from Germany for well over half a century," wrote Albert in his "Report" to the Wissenschaftskolleg on his academic activities during the period of October 1990 to June 1991 (box 5, folder 15), "I feel that the concepts I had shaped could provide me with a precious point of re-entry," And in "Exit, Voice, and the Fate of the GDR" (1995, p. 12), he explains that "the topic provided me with a point of reentry into German politics and history after an absence of over half a century from the country where I had spent my first eighteen years."

16 This, too, was probably the hidden ambition of a programmed *Colloque* at the Wissenschaftkolleg in Berlin, which was carefully prepared but did not take place because of Albert's ruinous fall in the French Alps in July 1995 (cf., below, ch. 3, n. 271, and ch. 4, n. 362).

connections with others, it is possible to verify, "record," and develop exit-voice theory, and to identify certain intellectual paths that will lead in the end to further concepts and clarifications useful for orienting ourselves in the world in which we live.

Moreover, after writing the sixth chapter of *The Rhetoric*, "From Reactionary to Progressive Rhetoric," as he explained in an interview for *Le Monde*,[17] "I looked in the history of philosophy for authors whose own development led them against themselves and their works, and then I remembered Nietzsche's celebrated *revirement* against Wagner—self-surpassing. That expression seemed a bit too grandiloquent when applied to me; I preferred the equivalent English self-subversion."

Observing Albert, then, in his self-subversions (which allow us to reconsider this or that aspect of his "magnus opus" right from its beginnings), my *Exercises* concern some aspects of his intellectual legacy (economic: chapter 2; political: chapter 3)—those few that I can address with clarifications and comments. These come together finally in chapter 4, "For a New Approach." Along with the analysis of texts and related information, this last chapter relies particularly on my own recollections (and participation) in order to delineate—as far as I understand it—the order of the problems to be faced, and also to interrogate the future on an issue that lies outside even Hirschman's agenda.

My exercises are simple theoretical "tests" that include a modestly programmatic task aimed at exploration, teaching, inspiration, and application.[18] In this sense they hark back to the *Exercises* of Joan Robinson (my illustrious supervisor in the distant 1960s). And they remind me (implicitly) that in part, Hirschman's work should be considered complementary to the "Keynesian revolution,"[19] which I long ago learned about firsthand from the group of talented economists who had gathered in Cambridge (U.K.) around John Maynard Keynes: Piero Sraffa, Joan Robinson, Richard Kahn, Nicolas Kaldor, Maurice Dobb, etc.

17 "Un entretien avec Albert Hirschman," in *Le Monde*, September 24–25, 1995 (box 72, folder 13).

18 I refer of course to Meldolesi (1994; English tr. 1995). In fact, although coming from a different visual angle, the argument picks up where I left off 30 years ago.

19 Hirschman (1981, p. 6). Indeed, seen from the point of view of the fight against unemployment, Hirschman's analysis "looks like a generalization of Keynes's problem, but from the point of view of its theoretical foundations, it deviates from it" (Meldolesi, 1995, p. 233, n. 9).

In preparing the present book, I was supported by the Hirschman Memorial at Princeton on March 24, 2013, and by a final stay at the Institute for Advanced Study in August 2013 that allowed me to examine a portion of the Albert O. Hirschman Papers now available at Princeton University's Seeley C. Mudd Manuscript Library. Previous versions of this paper have been published by Rubbettino, Italy (2014) and Universidad National de Quilmes, Argentina (2017).

· 1 ·

GENESIS OF A WATERSHED

(1) Barely six days after the fall of the Berlin Wall[20] on November 9, 1989, Henning Ritter published "Emigration, protest: on the topicality of a theory by A. O. Hirschman" in the *Frankfurter Allgemeine Zeitung*, an article that referred to *Exit, Voice, and Loyalty* (1970), which had been published in Germany in 1974 with the title *Abwanderung und Widerspruch* (*Emigration and Protest*). Faced with the difficulty of interpreting the extraordinary events that had led to the fall of the Wall, in other words, the then editor of the "social

20 I recall meeting Albert the day after the wall came down. It being the occasion of one of the numerous honorary degrees he received, it was my job, along with others, to open the ceremony at the University of Buenos Aires. I began by remarking in Italian that there could be no more auspicious day for giving Albert this recognition. The fall of the Berlin Wall had a very "special" significance for our "graduate," and it undoubtedly marked a decisive turning point in German and European history, with cross-pollinating consequences likely in all parts of the world (including Latin America). The public, composed largely of students, followed with interest what I had to say about international developments, but when I had to switch, for reasons of etiquette to the university "ritual" of speaking English, their disappointment was audible.

sciences" section of Germany's most influential newspaper had (surprisingly) decided to turn to the exit-voice model.[21]

The article sparked a lively debate in which a large group of intellectuals[22] took part, including Detlef Pollack, sociologist of religions at the University of Leipzig and direct witness to the events of autumn 1989. Pollack argued with authority that these contradicted Hirschman's model "to the extent that it asserts a predominantly rival, rather than complementary, relation between exit and voice in social processes."[23]

Albert Hirschman became aware of this debate when, at the age of 75, at the invitation of Wolf Lepenies, director of the Wissenschaftskolleg, he came to Berlin to spend the 1990–1991 academic year there.[24] "At that time, I was also able, through reading and interviewing, to become more closely acquainted with the history of the GDR and, in particular, with the remarkable story of its demise. Perhaps not surprisingly, I came to feel that the exit-voice perspective could indeed be of help in seeing some of the events in a new light and that it could itself be *enriched* by its encounter with a complex historical testing ground"[25] such as the unusual "fate" of East Germany.

In keeping with his characteristic intellectual style,[26] Albert did not feel he should participate directly in the debate (and possibly establish its rights

21 "The very fact that [these events] came as a total surprise to both spectators and actors," Hirschman commented, with his usual understatement, (Hirschman, 1995, p. 10) "suggests that our capacity to comprehend large-scale political and social change remains utterly underdeveloped. Under the circumstances, any conceptual tool [like 'exit' and 'voice'] that holds out the promise of providing a handle on the enigmatic events is likely to be eagerly seized." Naturally enough, one might think, but it was undoubtedly a favorable constellation of circumstances (from several points of view: interpretative, theoretical, proactive)—which led to Albert's participation (albeit belated and indirect) in these important "German affairs."

22 Hirschman (*ibid.*, p. 11) notes in particular papers by Detlef Pollack (1990a, 1990b), Christiane Heinze and Detlef Pollack (1990), Claus Offe (1990) and Wolfang Zapf (1991), to which he also adds those of Rogers Brubacker (1991) and John Torpey (1991)—two young U.S. researchers engaged in advanced studies at German universities.

23 Hirschman (1995, p. 11).

24 Albert's initial idea was to spend six months in Berlin. But then, in 1992, he returned to the Kolleg for another two months (and interviewed people on the events of 1989 at Leipzig and Dresden: cf., below, n. 56). Finally, in 1994, during his third stay in Berlin, he finished *A Propensity to Self-Subversion* (*ibid.*, p. 249, and 11–12).

25 Hirschman, *ibid.*, p. 12 (italics added).

26 It is a style which, as we shall discuss more fully below, avoids confrontation in order to preserve and develop its freedom of judgment and its own independent initiative; and which probably stems from his schooling and family upbringing (especially his relations

and wrongs through an "authentic" interpretation of his theory). Instead, in addition to making himself aware of why this discussion had come about[27] (and taking seriously, as we shall now see, its main analytical result), he raised scrupulous questions on two fronts. The first of these was how the exit-voice model could effectively help explain the facts, and the second was (vice versa) how the model could be further developed by its encounter with a historical chapter as engaging and complex as the events under discussion.

This gave rise to *Exit, Voice, and the Fate of the German Democratic Republic*, an "essay in conceptual history," written with the help of "some special lenses, in hopes of discerning new patterns, significant connections, and improved interpretations."[28] The text was highly successful in Germany and throughout the world,[29] and is one that I would like to revisit with care (regarding both interpretation and purpose) as a didactic exercise—but also as a way of introducing the broader intellectual landscape to be discussed further on.

Theory and Facts

(2) A recurring theme of *Exit*,[30] Hirschman recalled, "was the assertion that there is no pre-established harmony between exit and voice, that, to the

with his mother), and from his semi-clandestine (and clandestine) activities before and during World War II (Adelman, 2013, ch. 1–4; Meldolesi, 1995, ch. 1; and below, ch. 4).

27 Cf., above, n. 21.

28 Hirschman (1995, p. 41).

29 To give you an idea of this, I have chosen a letter dated August 22, 1992 (box 5, folder 12) from Elisabeth Pond, a journalist from the *Frankfurter Allgemeine Zeitung*, the influential German newspaper that, as I mentioned, had initiated the debate. "This is a letter from a 'fan,'" she writes, "[. . .]. As a German journalist I was present at a number of the demonstrations you describe [. . .]. I know how difficult it is to detect and interpret facts correctly. It seems to me that you have traced the change that occurred in the demonstrations very accurately. My congratulations." (The original version of the article, in German, "received the Thyssen Foundation Prize of 1992 for the best article [in that year] published in German by a social science journal").

30 Hirschman (1970). "To set the stage for my inquiry," Hirschman adds (i.e., for beginners), "it is useful to preset and reformulate as briefly as possible the concepts of exit and voice as they will be used here. They are two contrasting responses of consumers or members of organizations to what they sense as deterioration in the quality of the goods they buy or the services and benefits they receive. Exit is the act of simply leaving, generally because a better good or service or benefit is believed to be provided by another firm or organization. Indirectly and unintentionally exit can cause the deteriorating organization to improve its performance. Voice is the act of complaining or of organizing to complain or

contrary, they often work at cross-purposes and tend to undermine each other, in particular with exit undermining voice. Easy availability of exit was shown to be inimical to voice, for in comparison to exit, voice is costly in terms of effort and time. Moreover, to be effective, voice often requires group action and is thus subject to all the well-known difficulties of organization, representation, and free riding. By contrast, exit, when available, does not require any coordination with others."[31]

"In many situations," the author continues, "exit thus tends to undermine voice, particularly, so I argued, when exit deprives the potential carriers of voice of their most articulate and influential members, as is often the case." Hence the idea of a "basic seesaw pattern" between exit and voice—a "hydraulic" model, in other words, by which "deterioration generates the pressure of discontent, which will be channeled into voice or exit; the more pressure escapes through exit, the less is available to foment voice."[32]

Having thus briefly recalled this by now-classic development of the theme, Albert sets to work. "It is remarkable," he writes, surprisingly,[33] "that so primitive a model was able to account for as many diverse situations and experiences as have been marshaled by myself and others." This is a statement that at first glance seems perplexing. Why "so primitive a model," one wonders. Primitive compared to what? To economic models? The statement sounds out of place to anyone who knows the developmental process of Hirschman's thinking that led finally to the exit-voice "pattern," to its great versatility, to the unexpected intellectual interest it raised at the time (when *Exit* was published), the great debate that followed, the harvest of results achieved, etc.[34] For a "primitive"

to protest with the intention of achieving directly a recuperation of the quality that has been impaired. Much of my book and of my subsequent writings on this subject dealt with the conditions under which exit or voice or both are activated."

31 *Ibid.*, p. 12. "One of my principal points," the passage continues [still recalling the basics of the issue], is consequently that "the presence of the exit alternative can [. . .] *atrophy the development of the art of voice*" (1970, p. 43; original italics). "This inverse relationship between exit and voice was confirmed by numerous examples from economic and social life, such as those concerning the stock market, marriage, and the American workers' movement (1995, p. 13)."

32 *Ibid.*, p. 13. Albert had advanced this proposition in a well-known summarizing essay (originally conceived, as mentioned, for an entry in Vv.Aa., *The New Palgrave*, 1987) entitled "Exit and Voice. An Expanding Sphere of Influence" (Hirschman, 1986, ch. 4).

33 Hirschman (1995, p. 13).

34 I refer to the long gestation of Hirschman's exit-voice model, which put down roots during the author's "Colombian years," as well as to the impact (and substantial literature) that followed, as may easily be seen in the annual catalogs of citations or the summary essay

model, one might observe with a pinch of irony, isn't exit-voice . . . somewhat evolved?

"But [the model] could not be expected to be universally valid," Albert continues, "and indeed the events of 1989 in the GDR traced out a very different relationship" from what had been mostly studied up to that time. So that "primitive" as applied to the exit-voice "pattern" refers not to the model, but to the reality. And, in fact, it will become clear below that this essay (like the whole problem of self-subversion) fundamentally supports the inescapable necessity, for every social scientist, of adjusting thought to reality (rather than unreasonably claiming the inverse).

On the other hand, if we look at it from a different angle, we cannot help but admire the skill displayed in the argument. In fact, by acknowledging (emphasizing, in fact) the interpretive limitations of his own model, Albert dodges, *sic et simpiciter*, some of the (so-called "analytical") criticisms directed at him, without even having to name them. He also attracts the reader's attention by offering a foretaste of an appealing theoretical development (which he would later, as we shall see, take care to contain within narrow limits). And finally, he gives indirect credit to the (enduring) importance of the basic exit-voice model, marveling at the fact that, despite its so-called "primitive" nature, it has had so many applications.

(3) The reasoning thus opens to what is new, without at the same time having to disavow what has gone before.

"As was pointed out by an East German sociologist [Detlef Pollack]," Hirschman continues, "here [the case of the German Democratic Republic] exit (outmigration) and voice (protest demonstrations against the regime) worked in tandem and reinforced each other, achieving jointly the collapse of the regime." Alongside the seesaw or hydraulic pattern of exit- voice, an inverse logic begins to emerge (and conceptually assert itself)—their mutual reinforcement.

But this was not a bolt from the blue. Albert indeed recalls that he had *already* become aware of the need to complicate his basic model for some specific areas and cases, to the point of having recognized that expanding the opportunities for exit can sometimes "make for *more* rather than less participation and voice."[35] This, he adds, "*is indeed close* to how things worked out"

cited in n. 32 above (cf. Hirschman, 1970, 1981, ch. 9–12, and 1986, ch. 4; Meldolesi, 1995, ch. 6, and 2013, ch. 5; *Times Literary Supplement*, 1995).

35 For example, Hirschman writes, "I noted [in the cited above—cf. n. 32—summary essay 1986, p. 79] that since exit and voice are 'two basic complementary ingredients of democratic freedom, the right to exit and the right to voice have on the whole been enlarged

in the GDR in 1989.[36] But it by no means settles the question because the 40 years of East Germany's existence comprised "a large variety of exit-voice relationships."

In other words, while the debate (cf. sec. 1) was sparked by the apparent refutation of the exit-voice theory by events in the GDR in 1989, Hirschman maintained that, on the contrary, what some features of the original theory described was "close to how things worked out," but that in any case the entire span of the GDR's history was almost a "collection" of exit-voice relationships. "Some correspond faithfully to my original script; others depart from it more or less in the way that has just been sketched but will invite yet new interpretations."[37] This certainly does not put a damper on Pollack's observations or on the theoretical importance of historical events related to the dissolution of the GDR, but it does suggest that we take up the discussion starting *with the facts* (all the facts), and finally, to see if (and how) these facts can in turn enrich the theory.

Actually, there is a general, overall consensus that exit was antagonistic to voice in the entire postwar era preceding the events of 1989. Indeed, a comparison with the political history of Hungary, Czechoslovakia and Poland shows that while other relatively advanced Eastern European Soviet satellites fought "epic battles" against Communist domination (Hungary in 1956, the Prague Spring of 1968, the emergence of *Solidarność* in Poland in 1980), there was nothing similar in the GDR—with the exception of the premature and quickly suppressed worker insurrection of 1953. "The possibility of improving one's lot by just getting out—by moving to the other, bigger, freer, and soon to be more prosperous Germany—*fundamentally* distinguished the East German postwar experience from that of the Poles, Czechoslovaks, and Hungarians, who had

or restricted jointly.'" Moreover, concerning the question of school vouchers (*ibid*., p. 89), which we will come back to, he considered the possibility that "parents who have been passive because they were feeling powerless and fearing reprisal may feel empowered for the first time once they are given vouchers that can be used 'against' the schools currently attended by their children, and they will be readier than before to speak out with regard to desirable changes." Finally, "in describing the process of slave emancipation in Cuba in the late 19th century, Rebecca Scott has shown how slaves adopted at times a mixed, exit-*cum*-voice strategy" (Hirschman, 1995, p. 14, n. 5; original italics).

36 So that, Hirschman suggests, in contrast to what Detlef Pollack had written (cf., above, sec. 1 and n. 22), the events in the GDR in 1989 can actually be explained by the preexisting exit-voice theory. *ibid*., p. 14.

37 *Ibidem* (cf. previous note).

no such alternatives or prospects and who by and large were confined to their countries."[38]

In any case, and typically, this first general judgment is then "qualified (and limited)" by a look at postwar East-to-West emigration statistics. Apart from a 1953 "spike" (apparently due to the exceptional events of that year), the outflow to western Germany consistently fluctuated around a figure of two hundred thousand a year up until the Wall was built (1961)—promoted in the West by automatic citizenship in the Federal Republic of Germany for anyone from the GDR, and in the East by the idea that it was basically a pressure (and safety) valve.

But this last assessment was soon replaced by concern and alarm. In fact, "as it continued, the exodus of East Germans to the West—among them many highly skilled members of the labor force—came to be likened to a life-threatening hemorrhage that had to be stopped." The Wall was built, and this significantly reduced the flow of refugees.[39]

Nevertheless, the clandestine exodus remained in the thousands. Adding authorized emigrants (elderly people who were granted family reunification, expelled opponents and political prisoners ransomed by the FRG), we arrive at a total that fluctuates in the early years around 15% and thereafter around 10% of the previous flow.[40]

"What is actually surprising [. . .]," Hirschman comments, "is the extent to which the Berlin Wall and the assorted draconian border controls were *unable* to stop the emigration. [. . .] As a result, the hope for escape to the West was kept alive year after year by the *actual life experiences* of thousands of existing people" (to which must be added, of course, the ephemeral "vicarious mass escape" every evening, enabled by West German television broadcasts).[41]

(4) There are, however, *other reasons*—both "structural" and having to do with policy—that explain why the GDR was for many years "the most reliably tranquil as well as the most supine of the Soviet satellites."[42]

Concerning the structural reasons, it is in the first place true that unlike the Eastern Europeans around them, "the citizens of the East German rump

38 *Ibidem* (italics added).

39 *Ibid.*, p. 18.

40 Although "in the 1980s the flow swelled again, particularly in 1984, when large numbers of longtime applicants suddenly received permission to leave. Thereafter, the door was shut once again" (*ibid.*, p. 19).

41 *Ibid.* So that the reality (along with the mirage) of exit long continued to inhibit voice.

42 *Ibid.*, p. 15.

state could not look back on a sheltering history or national tradition of their own, nor did they have any established, more or less independent institutions (like the Catholic church of Poland) that would sustain them in a struggle for some autonomy from the all-powerful Communist Party and state."[43] In addition, by comparison with the other Soviet satellites, the GDR enjoyed a sort of "initial ideological advantage." In fact, there were many who, having been "first seduced and later disenchanted and perhaps appalled" by Nazism, sought to "forget the past or even atone" for old wrongs, and eagerly embraced the cleansing function of "the ersatz ideology or *Weltanschauung*" offered them by the Communist leadership.[44]

"Third, and probably most important, East Germany [. . .] was the front line of the extended Soviet empire in its contest with the West. It was in East Germany that the highest concentration of Russian troops and tanks was to be found, and it was there that the Soviet short-and medium-range atomic missiles were located." Therefore, given that the prospect of a nuclear exchange was "too awful to behold," and that "no one in his or her wildest dreams ever imagined that the Soviet empire would disintegrate from within," "the chances for successful voice were accordingly seen as being extremely low in East Germany, far more so than in less strategically situated areas."[45]

In conclusion, to understand the historical parabola of the GDR we must take into account not only the atrophying effect of exit on voice (the seesaw or hydraulic pattern), but also the *formidable obstacles* to voice ("that is, to any political movements of resistance or dissidence") that existed in East Germany at the time.

(5) Finally, as mentioned, there was *yet another source*—a policy source this time—that artificially muffled East German voice. "Throughout the forty-year existence of the GDR, authorities there showed every sign of being fully aware of the basic seesaw pattern of exit and voice. This is apparent from their frequent attempts to manipulate and exploit it. Particularly after they had substantially reduced exit by building the Wall, they realized that they could weaken internal opposition by a selective policy" that was more or less consensual. Poets, writers, actors and composers were expelled, dissidents were eliminated and

43 *ibid.*, p. 20. "Only at a fairly late stage did the Protestant church in East Germany take on that function to some extent." Nicoletta Stame and I actually saw this in an East Berlin hostel shortly after the fall of the Wall.

44 *Ibid.*

45 *ibid.*, p. 21.

the authorities regularly decapitated "opposition groups in their early stages [. . .] *without* having to resort to overt acts of heightened domestic repression." In addition, "many political opponents who [had landed] in prison" were "sold" to the Federal Republic, and so on. And since, "the people who were ransomed, expelled, 'let go,' or cajoled into leaving did not constitute compact, plotting, and therefore threatening exile communities," but instead "settled easily" in a variety of locations in the Federal Republic, "in the short term, the East German power-holders could justifiably feel that their policy of selective pushing out was both riskless and effective in reducing unwanted voice."[46]

This was true in the short term, but in the long run it didn't work out so well. The policy of selective expulsion in the end produced a decisive drain—the very "life-threatening hemorrhage" it was supposed to stop. In fact, when it came down to it, "the resulting exit-induced vacuum of leadership and of political life explains a good deal about the eventual collapse of the GDR as an independent entity and its easy absorption by the Federal Republic."[47]

Exit and Voice as Allies

(6) Albert thus approaches the heart of his interpretation.

The construction of the Wall reduced exit largely by changing it from a "feasible project" to "hope and fantasy." This, however, did not significantly increase voice (as the hydraulic model would have predicted), because at the same time it generated a parallel repression of voice. Indeed, "the decision to tear the city of Berlin asunder with a 165-kilometer-long wall, turning it into two non-communicating halves, was an extraordinary affirmation of state power that signaled the GDR's general readiness to be more aggressive against 'state enemies.'" [. . .] Under such conditions, "the increase in voice that might normally be expected when exit alone is curtailed did not and could not occur."[48]

46 *Ibid.*, pp. 22, 23 and 24.

47 *Ibid.*, p. 24. In Hungary, Czechoslovakia and Poland, Hirschman explains, "dissenters stayed put," and in time they "came to occupy a wide political spectrum from nationalism to liberalism to various social democratic tendencies. Hence, a pluralistic political discourse could evolve in these countries after the breakup of the Communist regimes in 1989. Not so in the GDR; here the most vocal opponents of the regime had been pushed out to the Federal Republic, where they had joined the existing political groups and had little interest in returning to the GDR."

48 *Ibid.*, p. 25.

Certainly, "the simultaneous repression of exit and voice in 1961 was to have its counterpart twenty-eight years later, when exit and voice exploded jointly and brought down the whole edifice of the GDR. At first glance, the events of 1989 look like the exact inverse of what happened, or failed to happen, after August 1961,"[49] in the sense that in both cases exit and voice moved in the same direction, contracting in the first case and expanding later.

But Hirschman was too skilled a social scientist (and too well schooled by experience) to build an elaborate theoretical framework on this basis that would "explain" such a reversal *sic et simpliciter.*[50] Rather, his purpose seems to me to be three-fold. First, he aims to lend more credence than he previously did to the mutually reinforcing nature of exit and voice operating alongside the well-known seesaw (or opposition). Second, he aims to bring back the mutually reinforcing nature within his already extensively-tested theoretical conception. And, finally, he seeks to enrich the seesaw (or opposition)—both as an "expanding sphere of influence"[51] and in its interpretive logic.

In fact, in the paragraph introducing the essay Hirschman had already written that rather than discouraging voice, exit could support voice—for example, through the allocation of school vouchers.[52]

49 *Ibid.*

50 "The German language has a peculiar gift for compact verbs, such as *umschlagen* and the famous Hegelian *aufheben*, which endow such turnabouts with *seeming reality*. I deliberately avoided these terms, as they evoke the famous dialectic, the 'negation of the negation,' and similar mysterious, if preordained, processes that dissolve all contrasts and reconcile all opposites" (*ibid.*, p. 43; italics added). Research, Hirschman seems to be saying, must shun like the plague such intellectual shortcuts, which do not correspond to actual facts. This of course implies the supremacy of reality over thought—the preference (where possible) for "brief" fact-thought concatenations and interactions, as opposed to "long" ones that are inevitably more problematic (and thus require a relatively higher level of verification). It also evokes the eternal Colornian "doubtfulness" (and consequent readiness to question, up to a point, previous findings). These are some crucial methodological cornerstones that will accompany us throughout the entire course of the argument.

51 Indeed, "An Expanding Sphere of Influence" is the subtitle of the 1986 summary article referred to above (cf., n. 32).

52 "Such a positive relation [. . .]," he had commented (1995, p. 14), "rests on a structure that is more complex than the one underlying the seesaw pattern. What happens here is that the newly won right to exit actually changes the human agents involved. Being allowed more choice, they become more aware of and more willing to explore the whole range of choices at their disposal. Once men and women have won the right to move about as they please, they may well start behaving in general as adult and hence as *vocal* members of their community."

Mutatis mutandis, this is the kind of change in human behavior that Albert seeks to pinpoint (and explain) as the direct cause of East Germany's "fate."

Actually, he writes,[53] "the inability of the GDR, starting in the spring 1989, to prevent a large-scale flight of its citizens to West Germany, via Hungary, Poland, or Czechoslovakia, signaled a novel, serious, and *general* decline in state authority. It was thus taken to imply a similar decline in the ability and readiness to repress voice—with the result that citizens started to demonstrate against the regime for the first time since June 1953. [. . .] This account of the collaboration of voice and exit in 1989 follows the lines of reasoning that have already been laid out in the introductory section.[54] There I suggested that when previously unavailable opportunities to exit are forced open, people may experience new feelings of empowerment. They might then consider or reconsider other options, including that of reacting to an odious state of affairs by a direct attempt at change—through voice—instead of flight."

(7) So the historical fate of the GDR is not a "brand new" kind of exit-voice interaction—one not yet considered by the theory, i.e., or outside its scope. And if it is instead the case that while the model of alliance and mutual reinforcement between exit and voice is undoubtedly less common "in nature" than the hydraulic model—even in the history of the GDR—it is also true that in the case of the breakup of East Germany, what took place was a sort of transformation, to use the classic expression, of quantity into quality. In other words, the historical event we are about to discuss was so important that it transformed the exit-voice relationship of connection and mutual reinforcement from an exception into a rule. "This sort of *conjunction* of exit and voice," Albert writes, "turned out to be exceptionally powerful in the German case and took some striking forms,"[55] such as would justify attributing a kind of "equal status" to the *alliance* between the economic mode of action (exit) and the political mode of action (voice), alongside the better-known opposition between them.

It is useful then to recall some of these forms briefly (with a view of later analyzing them in detail)—for their instructive uniqueness, certainly (in partly qualifying and redefining the scope of such an alliance), but also in order to identify the specific exit-voice paths that were taken (and their consequent interpretations). Also, finally—as we shall see further on—because there are additional lessons to be drawn from them.

53 *Ibid.*, pp. 25–26.
54 Cf. n. 52, above.
55 *Ibid.*, p. 26.

Of course, the events narrated (and interpreted) are part of a more general historical upheaval (which we cannot address here), that eventually led to the demise of the Communist system in Eastern Europe. Hirschman refers to this sporadically (only when he deems it essential), while here he presents as succinctly as possible the East German facts,[56] initially keeping exit and voice separate.

Exit—As early as 1988, a general effect of the way things had developed was a notable increase in the number of people who managed to find their way to the Federal Republic. In the spring of 1989, exits via Hungary intensified after the barbed-wire barriers along the border with Austria were removed. That summer the embassies in the GDR of the Federal Republic and the other surrounding countries filled with hundreds of East Germans seeking asylum. In September, Hungary officially opens its territory for transit into Austria. Meanwhile, the number of refugees in the embassies swells to thousands. The two German states reach an agreement to transfer these people across GDR territory to West Germany in special sealed trains.

Voice—In 1988 the Nikolaikirche, a church in central Leipzig, already a meeting place for "peace prayers," becomes a rallying point for people seeking to emigrate. In early 1989 it begins organizing assemblies, where the slogan "We want out" originates. In September a rival slogan begins to be heard—"We're staying here."[57] "For a while the *Ausreiser*, the partisans of exit, and the *Bleiber*, the partisans of voice, form separate, even somewhat antagonistic, groups. Eventually they merge under the slogan '*Wir* sind das Volk' (*we* are the people)."[58]

56 His careful reconstruction is of course based on numerous publications and accounts. "Interviews with Gerhard and Gudrun Rein and with Detlef Pollack in Berlin in early 1991," he writes (*ibid.*, p. 26, n. 14), "were most helpful. In May 1992 I spent several days in Leipzig and Dresden and talked with a number of participants in the 1989 events. I am greatly indebted to all of them."

57 "According to participant observers, a number of meanings were implied: 'We're staying here so as to make sure that things don't stay as they are'; or 'We're staying even though we don't like things here'; or 'You won't be able to get rid of *us*.' Despite the pervasive tension and fear, the back and forth of the two slogans—"we want out' and 'we're staying here'—introduces an element of entertaining street theater into the demonstration, which now emerges from the church and spills over into the adjoining streets." (*Ibid.*, p. 29).

58 This slogan, "particularly when the first word is accented, trenchantly denies the basic tenet of the Communist state's structure and ideology: that there is a complete identity of views and interests between the ruling Party and the population. This arresting slogan also seems to echo Bertolt Brecht's poem ['The Solution'] on the insurrection of June 17, 1953," which ends "Would it not be easier/ In that case for the government / To dissolve the people / And elect another?" (*Ibid.* and n. 19).

Another center of voice was Dresden, "the GDR's major rail and road gateway to Czechoslovakia, and from there to Hungary and the West. In September [1989] it fills up with many people from points west and north in the GDR—people who are planning to leave the country." On October 3 the Czechoslovak border is closed,[59] and the next day there are rumors that sealed trains carrying the refugees who had been camped in the embassies would cross the city headed for the West. "Large groups of would-be *Ausreiser* congregate in and around the main railroad station in hopes of somehow boarding these trains." This leads to the first demonstrations[60] (and the first riots), which then go on for several days. On October 8, "a young priest manages to obtain approval from a police official for the crowd to appoint representatives who will negotiate its demands with the authorities." "In the short span of five days," Hirschman concludes, "the Dresden crowd will have traveled all the way from a desperate push for exit to organized voice, complete with representation and delegation."[61]

(8) Interacting with exit, collective voice (not least thanks to the effect of the internal dynamic of the social movement that had developed in opposition to numerous attempts at repression) by now was pushing the GDR toward a point of no return.

On October 7, young people in East Berlin began to demonstrate as well—from the Alexanderplatz to the nearby Palace of the Republic, which was at

59 This marks a "fleeting, if influential, appearance" of the hydraulic model in the events of 1989 since—as Hirschman makes clear further on (*ibid.*, p. 34)—the prohibition of exit "contributed a great deal to the powerful development of voice in and about the Dresden railway station."

60 It was here that the two opposing slogans "We want out" and "We're staying here" were first heard. The origin of this second slogan seems to have been an appeal by a railway official—a woman—who, before the police intervened, tried to get the station cleared with the words: "'Citizens, go home—we promise you that all of you will be permitted to emigrate [*ausreisen*].' Whereupon a good many in the crowd, disbelieving such promises and unwilling to vacate the station, shouted back: '*Wir bleiben hier*'—we're staying right here! Only later, according to this account, did the meaning of the slogan change to the more sophisticated concept, 'we want to change things by staying.' Hence, voice may have arisen out of intended exit—not as a result of opposition to exit as such, but through linguistic ambiguity and slippage" (*ibid.*, p. 31).

61 *Ibid.*, p. 31. Indeed, at the same demonstration "delegates are somehow selected, and as they stand up, they are applauded by the seated crowd [on the cobblestones of a square in the vicinity of the station] by way of investiture. Thus is born the Dresden 'group of twenty,' which actually convenes with the mayor of Dresden the next day and works out concessions that lead to a relaxation of tensions."

the time hosting Gorbachev. On the 9th, in Leipzig, "the watershed event" took place that has been frequently referred to since as *Schicksaltag*—the fateful day. This was a demonstration involving circa 70,000 people, organized by four churches in the city center, in open defiance of the imminent threat of a crackdown in the style of Tienanmen Square in Beijing. "For all the tension of the situation on that Monday afternoon, the police do not intervene, no blood is shed—and the authority of the GDR is shattered forever. As one eyewitness [Christoph Wielepp] put it later: 'In the late evening of October 9, the GDR had become something different. This was obvious to all participants.'"

In fact, from then on there was an extraordinary acceleration of events. The border with Czechoslovakia was reopened. Honecker was forced to resign. On November 4, a gigantic demonstration of half a million people took place in East Berlin. On the 9th the Wall came down.[62] Eleven months later the GDR ceased to exist.

It is true, then, that exit-voice interaction in the 1989 events as a whole[63] is characterized by the phenomenon of *convergence*. "To appreciate the peculiarities of this situation," Hirschman argues,[64] it is helpful to recall that exit is "essentially a *private* and also typically a silent decision and activity. One can do it alone: there is no need to talk it over with anyone." And it is also "a private good in that it cannot be had through the exertions of others." "Voice," on the other hand, "is typically a *public* activity" that thrives "in concert with others [and on] delegation and all the other forms of collective action," and is subject, as known, to problems of free riding.

Thus "exit and voice have very different impulses, [. . .] they would seem to inhabit quite different worlds."

"How then," Albert asks, "did the two come to be so intimately bound up together during the events of 1989?" In response, he reflects on the steady trickle of exit to West Germany, long secret, smooth and quiet, and on how, in the 1980s, the phenomenon had become increasingly unbearable[65] to the religious, cultural and finally political consciousness of the country, to the point

62 The statistical data on East German emigration to the Federal Republic (*ibid.*, p. 27) correspond faithfully to the unfolding facts of 1989. They rise slightly, in fact, in the first months of the year, double between May and June and finally begin an explosive trend, one that from 21,000 people in August reaches 57,000 in October and 133,000 in November.

63 An exception to this largely prevailing trend was the reactivation of the hydraulic model produced by the closure of the border with Czechoslovakia: cf., above, n. 59.

64 Hirschman (1995, p. 34).

65 "This outmigration torments us already for many years [. . .]," declared, for example, Jens Reich, cofounder in 1989 of the citizens' movement Neue Forum (cit. in *ibid.*, p. 36). "[It]

of prompting it to oppose head-on, and successfully, the hateful key proposition of the regime's hard-liners ("we do not shed a single tear over those who leave") and to the point in all likelihood, of in this way averting the dreaded bloodbath.[66]

"There was something particularly devastating," the author concludes, "about these *silent*, *private* exits—they drove some of the more conscientious remaining citizens, such as Wolf, Reich, and Hein, to a passionate voicing of their concern and despair." And in September and October of 1989, Krenz and Schabowski helped drum up opposition to Honecher in the party's Politburo by arguing that "the exodus was a matter of great concern for the GDR and that every departure must be felt as a loss."[67]

(9) All well and good, one might observe. But how did things actually play out?

"A closer look reveals the sequence of events to be a variant of the way exit is usually supposed to work in alerting 'management' to its failings."[68] "In the case of the GDR," Hirschman explains,[69] "this straightforward feedback mechanism worked very poorly, because the managers of the GDR had inured themselves to it [. . .] and were in general an insensitive and inflexible bunch. But the mass exodus did sufficiently impress, depress, and alert some of the more loyal citizens [. . .]. The mobilization and voice of these citizens can be seen as a substitute for the failed response of the GDR managers or as a second wake-up call for them. The normal sequence of events that is supposed to be set off by exit has simply become more roundabout."

Finally, there is a second explanation, based on loyalty—which had been "shown to delay exit (as well as voice) when there was a decline in the performance of an organization," but which then, once a certain level of deterioration had been reached, stimulated a vigorous reaction from the interested parties. This way, if we "imagine an organization with two very different kinds of members, those with a great deal of loyalty and those with little or none, reactions to deterioration will take two distinct forms: those who are unburdened by

was so bitter, this feeling of sitting in the waiting room of a railroad station and everything around you is breaking loose. In the end it was unbearable."

66 *Ibid.*, p. 36.

67 *Ibid.*, p. 37. "This story," he states, "helps us understand how public voice was stimulated by private exit in the fall of 1989, instead of being undermined by it, as had been the case previously."

68 Generally, when customers abandon a company or members desert a party, the leaders of such organizations quickly realize this and usually run for cover.

69 Hirschman (1995, p. 37).

feelings of loyalty will be prone to exit, while the loyalists will resort to voice." The former are the *Ausreiser* (who favor exit) and the latter are the *Bleiber* (who support voice).[70]

And so we have two routes (that can be merged) for interpreting the events in the light of the Hirschmanian theory of exit and voice.

But that is not all there is to it. Actually, the author had already alluded to a general sort of explanation in the introduction to the essay (cf., above, sec. 6), comparing the events in East Germany in 1989 to the distribution of school vouchers. In this second case, the increased availability of exit indirectly induced a sort of empowerment of the citizens who benefited—a change in evaluation (and behavior) that stimulates voice. Evidently, something similar actually happened in that fatal year for GDR. "The real mystery of the 1989 events," Hirschman argues, "is the transformation of what started and was intended as a purely *private* activity [. . .] into a broad movement of *public* protest."

This is a theme that had drawn Albert's attention for a long time, perhaps always. He dedicated an important monograph to "shifting involvements" (to be discussed further on), which he doesn't mention here, perhaps in order to distance what he is about to write from his text of that time (and perhaps because of his rethinking of some of its fundamentals—which would lead him, eventually, to "mix the private and public spheres").[71] In any event, the explanation that follows in the text should be taken on its own, as an independent attempt to penetrate that complex issue—which of course makes it all the more interesting.

(10) "How and when," Hirschman asks,[72] "did public elements intrude upon the private sphere? How and when did they overwhelm the original intentions of the actors? The answer is contained in the historical account that has been presented." In essence, it is about being able to take in the minute lessons of events in stages.

"Originally the 1989 *Ausreiser* conceived their departure from the GDR as a totally private affair [. . .] in secret, silently, on tiptoe. But too many people had the same idea, and, as a result of external events such as the relaxation

70 *Ibid*., p. 38. "Although the concurrent emergence of these two distinct groups," Albert concludes, "could thus have been predicted from an elementary complication of my loyalty model, in fact the inventiveness of history was needed to suggest the complication and to reveal its importance."

71 I refer here to, respectively, to *Shifting Involvements* (1982) and to "Melding the Public and Private Sphere: Taking Commensality Seriously" (1998): cf., below, ch. 3.

72 Hirschman (1995, p. 39).

of frontier controls between Hungry and Austria, their moves were too successful to remain secret and private. Pictures of the exodus soon flooded the TV screens [. . .] making activists out of long-passive citizens. As a Protestant pastor of Leipzig said in November 1989, [. . .] 'the folks here said: . . . We won't go along [. . .] any longer.'"[73]

And moreover, "exit also ignited voice in another, more direct way" from within the ranks of the social movement that was beginning to form. "As the *Ausreiser* themselves converged at key points (border crossings, railroad stations, embassies), they realized they were no longer alone, recognized each other as being of similar mind, and *rejoiced in the community they had unwittingly forged*." Almost without realizing it, they themselves thus began a new experience that was collective and public. "The most remarkable episode of this sort was the massive occupation of the Dresden railroad station [. . .]. Upon looking at each other and particularly upon being told to clear the station, those erstwhile private Dresden *Ausreiser* went public. The very chant '*Wir wollen raus*' [We want out] turned them instantly from private to public citizens with a common cause. At this point those in the crowd who had no thought of leaving felt obliged to manifest their position in turn: '*Wirbleibenhier*' [We're staying here]."[74]

Two Observations[75]

(11) "It may look," Hirschman had written earlier[76] (cf., above, sec. 9), "as though the conjunction of exit and voice during 1989 in the GDR has been adequately

73 *Ibid.*

74 *Ibid.*, p. 39. "Such a tumultuous evolutionary process"—Hirschman adds—"can also be analyzed through the subsequent meanings attributed to the slogan '*Wir bleiben hier*' [We're staying here]. Initially it may have been a simple reflex, an automatic response to '*Wir wollen raus*' [We want out], without much else in the way of substance." Then, it "rather slowly and haltingly took on reformist meanings and messages." Its vagueness and ambiguity (cf. n. 60 above) perhaps made it effective because "everyone who intoned it could endow it with his or her own content." Furthermore, the slogan *Wis sind das Volk* [We are the people], which, as mentioned, ended up supplanting the two opposing pro-exit and pro-voice slogans, "inherited the ambiguity of '*Wir bleiben hier*' and was similarly enigmatic and vaguely threatening," until it changed into *Wir sind ein Volk* [We are *one* people], "a slogan that asked for the merger of the two Germanies and, implicitly, for the obliteration of the GDR" (*ibid.*, p. 40).

75 "The details of the story [of the GDR]," Hirschman declares (*ibid.*, p. 41), "are [. . .] its essence, but two general observations will provide a conclusion." (I shall consider them here in reverse order with respect to how they appear in the text).

76 *Ibid.*, p. 50.

explained" by two considerations—one concerning the effect produced by exit on the behavior of management and the other concerning the existence of two types of loyalty. "In the process, as expected, the theory has already been enriched by the historical events themselves," through a variant that is "more roundabout" than the normal sequence of events, in the first case, and through an "elementary complication" of the loyalty model, in the second.

"I should stop here, therefore," the author states. But this is not his intention since, as we have just seen, "the intimate fusion of exit and voice" that typified the protest movement in the GDR in his view "requires further comment." This then leads to a comparison with "my original [. . .] happy-end scenario." *Exit*, Albert recalled, "had been written with the 'constructive' purpose of exploring how exit and voice could help restore or nurture a faltering organization back to tolerable performance and health. Both exit and voice were seen primarily as mechanisms that would 'alert management to its failings' after a 'repairable lapse.' Yet it does not entirely exclude the possibility that an organization might actually fail to recover and instead succumb to the blows inflicted on it by exit and voice (as well as by its own weaknesses)."[77]

And this is exactly what happened. In fact, as we know, "the combination of massive exit and tumultuous voice in 1989 led to the death of the GDR rather than to its rebirth: that twofold critique, so long repressed, was simply too devastating to allow for any 'recuperation mechanism' to work. [. . .] The headlong rush to reunification was not to be halted. Indeed, the extinction of the German Democratic Republic can be seen as the ultimate penalty for the long suppression of both exit and voice."

Clearly, Hirschman is referring here to his initial model[78] and does not even allude to any further schemes or formulations—whether relating to some

77 *Ibid.*, p. 41. "I had argued," he goes on (original emphasis), "that exit and voice would yield the desired constructive results only if they came forth *with moderation*, thereby not only alerting management but also giving it the time needed to mend its ways. For the survival and recuperation of both business firms and political organizations, a mixture of 'alert and inert' citizens or customers would be far better, so I argued, than either total, permanent activism or total apathy" (see *Exit*, 1970, pp. 24 and 32).

78 Hirschman (1970). As mentioned above, this book, along with the 1986 summary article (cited, above, n. 32), is the only exit-voice text referenced in the essay we are discussing. The theoretical enrichment gained here—related to the exit-voice alliance being a logical "pendant" of their opposition, as well as to some specific points just mentioned—significant as it is, does not require, therefore, a formal change in the theory as initially in *Exit* (1970) that would modify, as (instead) it was suggested in the debate, the exit-voice relationship "from top to bottom." The theory was re-proposed in the 1986 article in relation to contemporary topics, so as to take into account the evolution of the literature on

sort of "reversal,"[79] or to oscillations, as in *Shifting Involvements*. On the contrary, its ultimate concern strikes me as the *opposite*—it is about the need to reconnect with reality and to prevent any kind of unwarranted manipulation of history by theory.

"I have attempted to give some shape," the author concludes,[80] "to the story of the short-lived German Democratic Republic by retelling it in terms of the contrasting categories of private exit and public voice. Such an enterprise runs the risk of making too much of a theoretical construct. In 1909 the French anthropologist Robert Hertz published an article about the extravagant extrapolation of the right-hand- left-hand dichotomy by language and culture to encompass ever more basic contrasts, such as right-wrong, divine-profane, and so forth. For quite some time, then, we have known about the strange proclivity of the human (or Western?) mind to exaggerate differences, to blow up what Hertz called an 'almost insignificant asymmetry' into unbridgeable binary oppositions—in short, to make socially constructed mountains out of natural molehills."

Here (finally!), Hirschman's propensity to "self-subversion" emerges. It does not, as we have seen, concern a criticism of the exit-voice theory as such—which is confirmed and actually developed by giving the exit-voice alliance similar importance to that of the hydraulic exit-voice opposition. Rather, it concerns *some of its applications*, which—Albert now realized—exposed it to the danger "of making too much of a theoretical construct." In fact, the passage continues, "I, too, may have engaged in this pastime [making mountains out of molehills] as I collected conclusive evidence for the existence in many realms of a fundamental antagonism between private exit and public voice." For those familiar with Hirschman's work, the "unnamed" work referred to here is undoubtedly *Shifting Involvements* (1982).[81]

"Here the German story of 1989," Albert continues, "stands as a reminder of Sportin' Life's[82] maxim, 'It ain't necessarily so'—a principle of theoretical

the subject. Simply put, this essay on the fate of the GDR adds a third "expository movement" to the previous two—the hydraulic model's opposition and co-presence on the one hand and the exit-voice alliance on the other—which effectively allows for the "vivisection" of an important page of contemporary history, and at the same time augments the typical forms of the theory's exposition.

79 Cf., above, n. 50.

80 Hirschman (1995, pp. 42–43).

81 Cf., below, ch. 3, where it will be seen how "Melding the Public and the Private Spheres: Taking Commensality Seriously" (1998) develops and generalizes this self-subversive starting point.

82 A character from George Gershwin's *Porgy and Bess*.

modesty that social scientists disregard at their peril. In some momentous constellations, so we have learned, exit can cooperate with voice, voice can emerge from exit, and exit can reinforce voice." In other words, we have learned that history can hide a whole series of unexpected relationships up its sleeve, and that theory, in order to be useful, must show great flexibility in adapting to such developments instead of claiming the reverse—that is, forcibly 'subsuming' (as the philosophers used to say) reality to theory.

(12) "The 1989 upheaval in the GDR," so begins the second conclusion,[83] "represents a reversal of a movement that has been held to be characteristic—disastrously characteristic—of German history. A great deal has been written about the propensity of Germans in various historical circumstances to retreat from the public domain to the strictly private—to the famous (or infamous) *innerlichkeit*. This movement is supposed to have come all too easily to Germans, particularly when they were confronted with distasteful and repugnant events in the public domain. The idea, often traced to Luther, that the inner, private sphere is something infinitely precious, pristine, and inviolable may indeed have undercut the emergence of the public citizen who assumes responsibility for the political life of his or her community. From this point of view, the story that has been told here provides a welcome counterpoint: it essentially chronicles how many East Germans found the road back from exit and apathy to voice, from withdrawal and purely private reaction to public action."

Here we begin to appreciate that the essay is interested not only in interpreting the events and testing (and enriching) the theory. What we also now see emerging, inevitably, is the need for a policy *sub speciae valutationis* reflecting the final outcome of 1989—a "happy ending" of great historical significance.[84] And what is more, by overturning "a movement that has been held to be characteristic—disastrously characteristic—of German history," such an outcome undoubtedly acquires greater value and opens new perspectives.

Even though the resulting movement in which many citizens took public action was "unintended [. . .] initially," Hirschman continues, "it became nevertheless a powerful and successful citizen movement. Thus it stands in contrast to the many failed revolutions as well as failures to resist tyranny that have marked German history since the Reformation."[85] "With their nonviolent

83 Hirschman (1995, pp. 41–42; cf., above, n. 75).

84 Which happened, however, as mentioned: cf., above, the beginning of sec. 11 and n. 77 in a way quite different from the "happy ending scenario" that had concluded *Exit*.

85 Hirschman (1995, p. 42). "It is therefore perhaps to be regretted," the passage goes on, "that language downgraded the movement from 'peaceful revolution' to *Wende* (turn) soon after it was over. Strangely, once Germans had finally succeeded in toppling, at considerable risk

actions," observed Richard von Weizsäcker, President of the Federal Republic, "the revolutionaries of the year 1989 have given all Germans a new awareness of liberty. The past is not extinguished in consequence. But a decisive new chapter has been added to our history"—a chapter, I would add, which may prove an invaluable guide to the future.

(13) "Albert," wrote Fernando Henrique Cardoso, "always sought to look at themes that seemed to hang at the margins or to examine facts that seemed unique or apart from the general course of things in order, through them, to illuminate a broader process, attaching more importance to interpretations with meaning than to insipid regularities. [. . .] In this manner are many of Hirschman's works: subjects appear as if they were minor, even though developed with precision, charm and grace. When finishing reading such books we are left with the correct impression that the analyses, suggestions and metaphors paved the way for the understanding of much broader processes than we were aware of at the beginning. Behind the apparent simplicity emerges, as if by chance, a sophisticated explanation."[86]

This is exactly right. Unified Germany and all of Europe have to be built on the absolute truth regarding a tragic past in which the German citizen, not least due to a lack of courage, accepted the crimes of Nazism and sank well below the limits of common day-to-day decency.[87] Now, however, the German reunification epic finally offers us a shining example of the defeat of the infamous *Innerlichkeit*, and a social resurgence[88] which, looking forward, can lay the foundations of a new democratic identity in Germany, Europe, and the entire Euro-Mediterranean area.[89]

but without major bloodshed, an oppressive and ruinous regime, they designated the event with a term that almost deliberately understated it. In this they resemble people who, on the basis of past missteps, have a poor self-image—when confronted by success in some new endeavor, they will strain to reinterpret that unfamiliar experience as yet another failure or, at best, as 'nothing to write home about.'"

86 Cardoso in VV.AA. (2013, pp. 15–16). "A good illustration of this"—he added—"was Hirschman's explanation of how it was possible for the Berliners to combine voice and exit in their struggle for the restoration of democracy. And there are many other findings which seem to refer to things of minor importance and yet, all of a sudden, the reader realizes that he is in the presence of exceptional heuristic tools."

87 Lepenies (2006, ch. 11).

88 Finally, this aspect of the question should be linked to another of Albert's essays, on the critique of communitarianism and the re-evaluation of conflict, which closes *A Propensity* and seems to want to make this resurgence permanent (cf., below, sec. 11, ch. 4).

89 At this point it seems to me that if Germany and Europe were to experience a real democratic impulse (participatory, reformist, productive, social, rejecting centralism, embracing

To conclude the conclusion, major events such as the fall of the Berlin Wall and the related nemesis of European Communism do not just represent a historical watershed between two epochs—they are also a ridge beyond which we can try to glimpse, in method and content, some of the contours of both the world we are in and the world to come.

What might be the effect, for example, on the construction of a unified Germany (and Europe), of this "new awareness of liberty" triggered in 1989 (which followed, it should be mentioned, the revolt of the young against parents who had accepted Nazism)? Doesn't it perhaps respond to a need to renew our continent? And point to new policy needs?[90] If the answer is affirmative, then we need to understand still better what happened in the "events of 1989"—what actually happened in events that "were not experienced [by the protagonists] as stemming from an enigmatic turnabout in the functioning of social processes."[91]

"Those who lived through them," Albert adds with a hint of self-irony, "*were not troubled at all* by the fact that exit and voice now worked hand in glove after having undermined each other for four decades. A problem arises only for the social scientist who seeks a deeper understanding and who, in the course of this attempt, fashions a conceptual framework that initially makes it easier, but subsequently can make it more complicated, to understand what is going on."[92] Unless of course, as mentioned, she or he comes armed with "a principle of theoretical modesty" ("it ain't necessarily so") that allows a concrete re-connection with the lessons of the events.

social justice) and ascendant in the sense of a United States of Europe, Mediterranean, and Middle Eastern problems might also appear in a different light.

90 Which of course will not come as a surprise, since this is Hirschman—an author for whom analysis and policy should move forward together, hand in hand.

91 Hirschman (1995, p. 43).

92 *Ibid.* (emphasis added). Resurfacing here, evidently, is the dispute with theoretical language (such as that of philosophical Idealism and Marxism, which he had encountered in his youth), which at first glance appears "enlightening," but then turns out to be "imprisoning." (Adelman, 2013, ch. 2 and 3). "In that case, of course, our analyst may still come out on top by showing how instructive it is that events should have diverged from the original scheme!" Still, the point remains—it is essential to adjust thinking to reality (and not vice versa).

· 2 ·

ON THE ECONOMICS LEGACY

(1) Hirschman's last essay, written initially for a conference at Harvard, is entitled "Fifty Years After the Marshall Plan: Two Posthumous Memoirs and Some Personal Recollections." It is an instructive text—meant to provide both a better understanding of Albert's personal postwar story[93] and a way of approaching

93 In answer to the question how he had managed to conceive *The Strategy* (1958), Albert Hirschman long responded with the most famous of his "half-truths"— that he had gone to Colombia "without any prior knowledge of, or reading about, economic development. This," he added, "turned out to be a real advantage; I looked at 'reality' without theoretical preconceptions of any kind. Then, when I returned to the United States after four and a half years' intensive experience as an official adviser and private consultant, I began to read up on the literature and discovered I had acquired a point of view of my own that was considerably at odds with current doctrines" (1984, 1986, p. 5). Following these words, he finally admitted *coram populo* that he had previously worked on the Marshall Plan for the Federal Reserve Board. But as we shall now see, only 15 years later, in the 1998 essay which we are about to consider, some of the key reasons behind his "transition" between the two experiences—from "Euro-American" to "Colombian"—may be truly understood. This suggests a collateral observation. If, for a number of reasons (of character, education, eternal temptation, experience, basically stateless personal condition, etc.) Hirschman always had some difficulty in clarifying fully how things actually are, this state of affairs (Meldolesi, 2013, p. 93) is not likely to help us understand his work, and it undoubtedly prompts critics to multiply their efforts at clarification.

his remarkable elaboration of his ideas. It in fact concerns the author's role during that period (mainly in Washington and France), and suggests new ideas about the origin of *The Strategy of Economic Development*.[94]

The two books of memoirs referred to in the title of the essay are by Robert Marjolin and Richard Bissell.[95] Hirschman had known Marjolin before the war, when he wrote a series of articles on the Italian economy for Marjolin's *L'Activité Economique*,[96] and came across him again, as Jean Monnet's right-hand man in French planning and as secretary general of the Marshall Plan's Organization for European Economic Cooperation (OEEC).[97] Bissell, on the other hand, had a key role at the Economic Cooperation Administration (ECA), with Paul Hoffman, the automobile manufacturer appointed in 1948 as the first Marshall Plan Administrator.[98]

94 Having recently written about the Italian aspect of this genesis (Meldolesi, 2013, ch. 3), I can say that this last essay of Albert's seems to me particularly useful in rounding out the reasoning from the Euro-American side. Proceeding in stages, it ultimately leads to a more reasonable and balanced understanding of the different aspects of its postwar formulation.

95 Since both books are posthumous, the titles were not chosen by the authors. It so happened that Marjolin's—*Le Travail d'une vie* (1986)—turned out to be appropriate, while the title of the book by Bissell (a Republican-oriented MIT economics professor on long-term loan to the Administration), *Reflections of a Cold Warrior* (1996), chosen by Yale University Press, was much less so. The title in fact reflects several subsequent phases in Bissell's life that would "eclipse, for the general public in the United States, the remarkable role Bissell had played earlier in Europe. But those who knew him at the time," Hirschman argued (1998, p. 35), "tend rather to agree with what he wrote himself in introducing his own brilliant chapter on the Marshall Plan: 'The challenge and stimulation I knew I would experience convinced me to postpone academia. . . [W]hat followed were perhaps the most worthwhile years of my career.'"

96 "I met Marjolin first in Paris, in 1938, when Mussolini's new anti-Semitic decrees compelled me to return to France after two years in Italy. [. . .] I was twenty-three years old, and Marjolin gave me my first job as the Italian specialist of *L'Activité Economique*, a quarterly review on recent economic trends in Europe, which he published for the new Rockefeller Foundation," (cf. Adelman, 2013, ch. 5; Meldolesi, 1995, ch. 1).

97 Hirschman (1998, p. 34). "Marjolin was appointed secretary general and was in fact the guiding spirit of the Organization for European Economic Cooperation (OEEC) from 1946 to 1955 and later became vice president of the European Economic Community, from 1958 to 1967."

98 Hoffman, who as the first Marshall Plan Administrator was director of the ECA, "asked Bissell to join him as the deputy and assistant administrator for programs. Bissell became the recognized intellectual leader [of the ECA] and a forceful spokesman for the agency during congressional hearings for the organization" (Hirschman, 1998, pp. 34–35).

Regarding Bissell, Marjolin wrote that "his considerable intellectual abilities and the warmth of his feelings toward Europe contributed a great deal to the success of the enterprise." And referring to his collaborators, he added, "Never in my experience, before and after the Marshall Plan, have I known an international team animated by such an intense desire to achieve success in a common enterprise."[99]

In Washington, Bissell had gathered around him a small group of especially talented and active young economists to debate the key issues in the reconstruction and revitalization of Europe. "I soon discovered," Hirschman wrote,[100] "that to do my job [with the Federal Reserve Board, on some aspects of the Marshall Plan] adequately, I had better get to know the actual policy makers in this area in Washington. They were a small group of people around Bissell, a so-called brain trust, which fed various new institutional ideas to him, and through him to the Paris office of the new Marshall Plan agency, the ECA. I became quite friendly with this group, whose original members were Van (Harold Van Buren) Cleveland and Ted (Theodore) Geiger. Later on, this group was joined by another young man, John Hulley. I came to spend a good deal of time with these people, so that my office was virtually transplanted from the Federal Reserve Board to the new ECA building. I much enjoyed taking part in this manner in the 'activism' of this group, which constantly invented new functions for the Marshall Plan and its dollars."

At the Dawn of Contemporary Europe

(2) For anyone who has racked their brains as I have over Hirschman's scholarly work during that period,[101] the passage just quoted has an unprecedented and fairly revealing "sound" to it, because it allows us to account for (and begin to mentally sort out) the more than 40 articles the author drafted at that time.

In fact, as Albert recalls, there were basically three areas of focus under the Marshall Plan. First, "the Western European countries were to get together and to present jointly an estimate of the help that was needed from the United

99 Marjolin (1986, p. 196; cit. in Hirschman, 1998, p. 37).

100 *Ibid.*, pp. 38–39. In 1946 Albert began working for the Federal Reserve Board in Washington where, he writes (*ibid.*, p. 38), "it was my initial task to follow economic and financial events in France and Italy. I soon became responsible for Western Europe as a whole, and to the extent the Federal Reserve had a role in U.S. foreign economic policy, the Marshall Plan became my area of competence."

101 Meldolesi (1987, 1990, 1995, ch. 1, 2013, ch. 3).

States. This task was accomplished fairly rapidly: the Committee of European Economic Cooperation (CEEC) was formed in Paris and it completed its report by September 1947. With the [U.S.] Congress passing the needed authorization and appropriations, large-scale aid was flowing to Europe by the middle of 1948."[102]

"The second important area" was the European Payments Union, "in whose negotiation," Hirschman writes, "I became deeply involved." "In particular, I became interested in the plans for Intra-European Payments and in the various attempts to move away from the strict bilateral channels to which trade and payments in Europe were then still confined."[103]

The third task was "the reconstruction of multilateral trade in Europe. Here, in principle, the idea was again that the Europeans should come forward with a joint proposal for what was called, rather ambiguously, the further 'integration' of Europe."[104]

With all this in mind, let us now return to Albert's writings from the period. Several things immediately become clear. In the first place, many of the texts pertain to the "initial task" he was given, "to follow economic and financial events in France and Italy."[105] Second, the small group of writings concerning the European Payments Union is very significant,[106] and among these a text of limited circulation, extraordinarily prescient, stands out—"Proposal for a European Monetary Authority," about which we shall now speak. Finally, concerning the reconstruction of multilateral commerce in Europe, there is a lecture Hirschman gave at the State Department ("Approaches to Multilateralism and European Integration") that undoubtedly takes on a "special" significance from our point of view.

That is to say that having at one time (1990) edited the publication in Italian of the last two papers mentioned above, I have always seen these "visionary" texts (for their specific relevance and historical importance even in retrospect, and because of the unusual fact that they had remained unpublished until then) as standing out from the rest of Albert's scientific work at

102 Hirschman (1998, p. 38).

103 *Ibid.*, pp. 37 and 38.

104 *Ibid.*, p. 38. "But, by this time, the Marshall plan agency in Washington and its new Paris branch had come into flourishing bureaucratic existence and they, together with what had now been renamed the Office of European Economic Cooperation (OEEC) in Paris, participated fully in the 'idea mongering' that went on in various attempts to come forward with the best conceivable formulas."

105 Cf., above, n. 100.

106 Albert considered this his main occupation at the time.

the time—which, while truly creative and ingenious, inevitably fell within the scope of the work assigned to him.[107]

Now, finally, I think I understand *why*.

(3) Let us look at the details.[108] "As an example," Hirschman wrote, "I will recall that, back in December 1949, I prepared a paper entitled 'Proposal for a European Monetary Authority,' where I presented a fairly detailed survey of the common fiscal, monetary, and foreign exchange policies that might be adopted gradually under the guidance of a future European Central Bank."

In this essay Hirschman asked "whether it is possible to think of forms of monetary and financial organization for Europe that do not ask for the impossible, yet which would result in a closely knit European monetary and financial structure."[109] In answer he examined in detail the functions of a hypothetical "Authority" which, starting from existing national sovereignty constraints, might by degrees acquire powers to coordinate monetary and fiscal policies, reserves, exchange controls, service functions, etc.

"The paper," Albert recalled in 1998, "was circulated within the ECA. A note written by Van Cleveland introduced me as a staff member of the Federal Reserve Board and explained that the paper was circulated 'in response to an informal request.' Cleveland was a member of our brain trust and was identified in his note as 'program secretary' in the ECA. The note also took

107 In his papers from this period there are at least two lines of reasoning, one concerning countries (mainly Italy and France), and the other concerning European integration. Moreover, Hirschman's 39 texts from the *Review of Foreign Developments* (the internal bulletin of the international division of the Federal Reserve Board) can be organized into two groups: "informative (relating to trade flows and the system of payments between European countries) and proactive. The latter reflect an effort to put forward proposals tailored to important specific needs—as in the case of external purchase, the allocation of unused entitlements, and the liberalization of the Eca dollar [. . .]—and they also reflect the need to find common ground between conflicting interests as the possible basis of agreement for the European Payments Union (which would later play a significant role in the negotiation and its successful outcome)" (Meldolesi, 1990, pp. xii and xv). Some of these texts were republished (in Italian) in Albert O. Hirschman, *Potenza nazionale e commercio estero* (1987), Pier Francesco Asso and Marcello de Cecco, eds; and in English in Albert O. Hirschman, *The Postwar Economic Order* (2023), Michele Alacevich and Pier Francesco Asso eds. (My comments are in the works cited in n. 101).

108 Hirschman (1998, p. 39). "This paper," Albert wrote in parentheses in the text, "has not been published, except for an Italian translation, 'Proposta per una Autorità Monetaria Europea'" (see Meldolesi, ed.1990, pp. 7–18).

109 Hirschman (1990, p. 8).

care to add that the views expressed were 'not necessarily those of the Federal Reserve Board.' "[110]

In addition, as a second example (or rather, as an informal contribution to the third task of the Marshall Plan mentioned above—"the reconstruction of multilateral trade in Europe"), Albert could have pointed to[111] the cited 1950 conference lecture, "Approaches to Multilateralism and European Integration"—used in typescript as teaching material by the Foreign Service Institute of the Department of State—in which Hirschman took a position, *apertis verbis*, favoring discrimination against American goods (that were not complementary to European goods).[112]

In fact, strikingly foreshadowing an important feature of the progressive construction of the European Common Market, Albert (introduced here as the Head of the Western European Section of the Federal Reserve Board's Division of Research and Statistics), asserts that the expansion of trade among European countries would spur their industries to achieve higher productive efficiency—this through greater adaptability and mobility of resources, better exploitation of economies of scale, and above all the development of competition, initiative and European "morale" (i.e., the unleashing of Europe's socioeconomic vitality).

This, he argued, would in turn reinforce the competitive position of European countries in the global market, allowing them in effect to overcome their "dollar scarcity." Critics of European integration—Albert explains at this point

110 Hirschman (1998, p. 39). This was actually a "Memorandum," labeled "Confidential," that was circulated privately by H. Van B. Cleveland, "Program Secretary" of the Economic Cooperation Organization (ECA)—partly so that it could be discussed by officials engaged in Program Coordination on Fiscal and Trade Policy, which then came under the Marshall Plan.

111 But he did not. Probably a sign that Albert's later caution about this essay was greater than that exercised to "protect" "Proposal for a European Monetary Authority" (see n. 108). Even in 1998, it seems, Hirschman thought it preferable to avoid talking about it, probably as a precaution. (But it is also true that the Common Market was by then an established fact, while the birth of the Euro was still a topical issue).

112 This text, published at the time only in Italian in Hirschman (1990), reverses a view Albert had expressed publicly in the second part of "Disinflation, Discrimination and the Dollar Shortage" (1948b). It is notable that along with rethinking this point, what he actually held to be true was only made public 40 years after its publication (which in addition had been in Italian, rendering it not readily accessible to the standard researcher). Furthermore, perhaps to throw off any snooping, the 1998 Albert doesn't even cite the lecture (cf. n. 111).

with a felicitous *reductio ad absurdum*[113]—claim that progressively decreasing customs barriers would produce a worsening dollar shortage—in which case they should also advocate increased barriers and further European fragmentation. "It is doubtless true that if the province of Champagne were separated by high tariffs from the rest of France some champagne that is now consumed in Paris would be shipped to New York. But it will probably be conceded that the destruction of the previous integration between the province of Champagne and the rest of France would weaken the viability of the whole area by far more than by the worth of such an increase in champagne sales in the U.S."[114]

(4) These plainly plausible ideas and proposals—which retrospectively assume historical importance in the formation of the economic thinking that enabled the birth of contemporary Europe—were at the time addressed to the people in the American administration who were favorable toward European integration.[115]

It all makes sense, one might argue, but how did the Hirschman of that time "see it the way did"? Working for the Federal Reserve Board, shouldn't he have followed the dictates of the institution?

Well, we finally have some prominent "finds" that can answer this question. I will limit myself to two.

First, for a sense of the atmosphere (positive and negative) at the time, it should suffice to cite an exceptional witness—Jean Monnet. Finding himself in the United States in April 1948, at the beginning of the Cold War, Monnet writes, among other things, in his *Mémoires*: "Accustomed as I was to the American temperament, I was disturbed at so strong a will to act and so great an impatience to see a convalescent Europe stand on its own feet. These seemed likely to lead to instability and future misunderstanding." As he wrote to Robert Schuman, "I cannot but be struck by the relationship that threatens to develop between this great and dynamic nation and the countries of Europe, if they remain as they are, in their present state of mind." And in effect it was true, as we shall see later, that even with all the limitations of the case, the preliminary elements of the future European Community were being articulated

113 Which might sound rather odd to an American nationalist ear: see, above, ns. 111 and 112.

114 Hirschman (1990, pp. 32–33).

115 Obviously, the author was ahead of his time—both on the material side, from which the Common Market would emerge, and on the monetary side, which would lead to the Euro. It will be noted, however, that in spite of its extraordinary success, the European Central Bank unfortunately still does not perform all the functions of the European Monetary Authority proposed by Albert Hirschman back in 1949.

at that time under the impetus of this "impatience," and they prompted Monnet to envision a sort of Western federation.[116]

For the second point I will return to the 1998 text with this particular aspect of the situation at the time in mind. "The most important function of our group[117] [around Bissell] was to work on a plan for setting up and improving a new intra-European payments scheme—the European Payments Union, soon to be known as EPU. At an early stage I did not realize that this activity would eventually produce a conflict between my new role as informal adviser to the ECA and my bureaucratic position as a staff member of the Federal Reserve Board."

In other words, we learn that in addition to its impatience (a kind of "rage de vouloir conclure" of Flaubertian memory), the American government was also split, and that this conflict was having an effect on practical work. While the ECA, in agreement with the State Department, had taken on board the pro-European will to action aiming to see Europe stand on its own feet noted by Monnet, Hirschman's immediate superiors at the Federal Reserve saw things differently.

"The international division of the board to which I belonged," Albert wrote,[118] "was headed first by Frank Southard, who later became the U.S. representative on the executive board of the International Monetary Fund (IMF), and then by Arthur Marget. Both men were highly critical of the new functions that the ECA was proposing for the European Payments Union and which they saw as conflicting with the principles and expected role of the International Monetary Fund. By the time the positions of the various U.S. agencies participating in international economic policy making (the members of the National Advisory Council for International Monetary and Financial Affairs) had become clear, my point of view coincided with that of the ECA."

So, on this crucial point, Albert sided *against* his superiors. In fact, the ECA "wholly supported the European Payments Union, but was opposed vehemently

116 Monnet (1976; English tr. 1978, pp. 272–273). "In my opinion," Monnet continues, "Europe cannot long afford to remain almost exclusively dependent on American credit for her security, without harmful results both here and in Europe. Everything I have seen and reflected on here leads me to a conclusion which is now my profound conviction: that to tackle the present situation, to face the dangers that threaten us, and to match the American effort, the countries of Western Europe must turn their national efforts into a truly European effort. This will be possible only through a *federation* of the West" (original emphasis).

117 Hirschman (1998, pp. 39–40).

118 *Ibid.*, p. 40

by the Treasury and, to a somewhat smaller degree, by the Federal Reserve. In the end, the Economic Cooperation Administration view prevailed, largely because Paul Hoffman's role [in the Marshall Plan] was paramount. In October 1949, he had gone to Paris to deliver a rousing speech in which he appealed to the need for European 'integration' no less than fifteen times, as Bissel emphatically points out.[119] With the European Payments Union standing as the current symbol for 'integration,' it won out over the doubters and skeptics."[120]

(5) Hence, in spite of the opposition of his superiors, and acting on the side of the United States, Albert had managed to make a major pro-European and "federalizing" contribution—in both thought and action—to the construction of the new Europe. He had taken part firsthand in a process which, as we shall now see, had major consequences *far beyond* the mere (although necessary) distribution of the loaves and fishes of the Marshall Plan.

This is a revealing admission that plainly corrects and completes what Hirschman had written in "A Dissenter's Confession" (1984) and in the texts collected by Asso and de Cecco in *Potenza nazionale* (1987). In other words, he had found himself operating among ideologized economists—orthodox and Keynesian—and had made every effort in his work to undermine their certainties (and to head off the use of the undue power that American technicians often attributed to themselves). Albert's work—as we can now see (more and better than before)[121]—also had an important explicit and forward-looking *construens* side, carried out in concert with a group of young economists gathered

119 Bissell (1996, p. 63; cit. in Hirschman, 1998, p. 40).

120 *Ibid.*

121 We knew, in fact, that on the American side Hirschman had been involved in the study and negotiation of some inter-European payment schemes, but not knowing what was going on "behind the scenes," we could not even guess at the historical truth of the matter as a whole. Indeed, in retrospect, I can say even more. The fact is that even though I dealt on several occasions with the younger Albert's development (cf. the texts cited in n. 101); even though I took pains each time to show Hirschman what I had written before publishing it; even though some of these writings were translated into English, Spanish, and French; and even though for years on end I collaborated with the author, he never mentioned the matter to me. I can only suppose, in this regard, that his natural reserve, which had developed into a somewhat conspiratorial attitude at the time of his prewar anti-fascist activities, turned into tomb-like silence on this aspect of the time of the Marshall Plan (and even more so of McCarthyism), and that he finally decided to reveal the infighting at that time within the U.S. government, which he had taken part in, only *after* the passions and heat of the Cold War era had thankfully lost steam.

around Bissell at the ECA, which ultimately resulted in an extraordinary and immediate outcome—the European Payments Union.[122]

On the other hand, considering the roots in method and content that were formed (mainly) in dialogue with Eugenio Colorni in Trieste in 1937–1938, and the federalist option he had developed, at a world level, in *National Power* (1945),[123] it seems to me entirely logical that during the years of the Marshall Plan Hirschman was comfortable favoring, in a sense, the great "federalizing" thrust in Western Europe coming at the time from the United States, in the wake of the tragedies of the recently concluded war (and facing the dangers of the Cold War that had just begun).[124]

"If we now look," the 1998 Hirschman continues, "at the views on the European Payments Union as expressed by Bissell and Marjolin a considerable time after the events, we are struck by how strongly favorable their opinion has remained. Bissell wrote: '[. . .] the EPU created a clearing mechanism for payments made in any European currency. With all European currencies readily transferable, the barriers of bilateral trade arrangements were broken [. . .]. I have always felt that *the EPU was in some ways the supreme organizational achievement of the Marshall Plan*.'"[125]

"As for Marjolin, his admiration for the American (i.e., ECA) initiative in pushing the European Payments Union through is even more striking. He writes: [. . .] 'Not only did the United States grant at the time massive financial aid [. . .] but it pushed and jostled the Europeans to unite and to increase in this way their economic and political strength. To be more precise, the United States pushed the European countries to create a system of payments which

122 That Albert reveals all this only at the end of his long scientific career speaks volumes about the rationale behind his "half-truths"—his characteristic "telling and not telling." It was a mixture of stateless prudence, personal confidentiality and the expediency of the "half-silence"—true or presumed: see, above, ns. 93, 112, and 121.

123 Independently, but in parallel with Eugenio Colorni's Introduction to the *Ventotene Manifesto* (1944; cf. Meldolesi, 1995, ch. 1, and 2013, ch. 3).

124 Meldolesi (2013, ch. 2). In retrospect, this might help us understand why Albert, almost handing us a previously unknown key to the puzzle, chose as we have seen to publish in Italian (but not in English) the two unpublished essays from the Marshall Plan era that we are discussing—in *Tre Continenti* (1990), a collection that grew out of his honorary degree from Turin where, in his acceptance speech, he provided an extraordinarily vivid and interesting glimpse into his prewar association with Eugenio Colorni in Trieste. In any case, this in no way justifies, on either a political or professional level, Jeremy Adelman's (2013, p. 701) omission of these two key essays from the list of the author's articles in his maxi-biography—*Worldly Philosopher. The Odyssey of Albert Hirschman*.

125 Hirschman (1998, pp. 40–41) and Bissell (1996, p. 64). Emphasis added by Hirschman.

restored the convertibility of their currencies into each other while excluding the convertibility of these currencies into the dollar. Even more, the United States virtually forced the Europeans to free a considerable portion of their imports from other European countries while accepting that import restrictions on the same products be maintained when they originated in the United States. This way of acting unselfishly, *while apparently absurd*, would bear its fruits. In the course of the fifties, Europe's payments to the rest of the world could increasingly be paid without recourse to American aid until general convertibility, including the dollar, could be restored in 1958. Progressively, the discriminatory measures against American foreign trade would be abolished . . . The sort of *wager* the Americans had made in the last ten years had therefore been won. In the course of history, it is rare to see the long-term and highly uncertain benefits accrue so neatly.' "[126]

More on the Genesis and Nature of *The Strategy*

(6) But there was still the other side of the coin. The ECA's action, Bissell explained, was taken "in total disregard of standing U.S. policy, which strongly supported multilateralism," and therefore strongly opposed any discrimination against American goods. The ECA initiative was thus undertaken "in spite of opposition from the Treasury, which understandably was *infuriated*."[127]

"This exception to the rule of nondiscrimination," Albert comments, "explains also why the arrangement [of the European Payments Union] aroused such unremitting hostility on the part of some sections of our own government, not to speak of the recently created International Monetary Fund." On the other hand, he adds, concluding his argument, Marjolin "points to the direct connection between the Marshall Plan and the European Payments Union, on the one hand, and the Treaty of Rome and the European Customs Union ten years later.[128] Today these positive appraisals of the European Payments Union by Bissell and Marjolin make me feel good. But at the same time,

126 Hirschman (1998, pp. 41–42) and Marjolin (1986, pp. 217–218). Emphasis added by Hirschman. "Viewed from this angle," Albert comments (1998, p. 42), "it was a different and higher form of altruism than simple commodity aid, which had been the essence of Marshall aid. It permitted and encouraged temporary discrimination against imports from the United States."

127 *Ibid.*, p. 41 and Bissell (1996, p. 65). Emphasis added by Hirschman.

128 Hirschman (1998, p. 42) and Marjolin (1986, pp. 220–221).

my personal position was becoming ever more difficult. As Bissell remarked, the United States had pushed through a policy that "infuriated" not only the Treasury, but also its allies within the government such as the Federal Reserve, where I was still working. The positions I had taken made me feel increasingly uncomfortable.[129] When, after a while, the opportunity arose to leave Washington, I seized it with much relief. Recommended by the World Bank, I decided to move to Bogotá, Colombia, as an economic and financial adviser to the government there. Little did I appreciate then how this move would start an entirely new phase of my life."[130]

The affair is thus an unprecedented and very useful element in our understanding of the genesis of The Strategy of *Economic Development* (1958). I knew, in fact, that at the end of the Marshall Plan Hirschman had looked around for a new job. He had ruled out any comfortable accommodation with an international organization in Washington or Paris. He had developed an interest (as yet embryonic) in problems of development in underdeveloped countries. He had explored the possibility of moving to Portici (Naples) or somewhere else in Italy.[131] Then he decided on Colombia—a courageous decision that would also prove to be pioneering and fortunate despite the difficulties. Yet, not knowing *apertis verbis* of the matter just recalled, I could hardly have guessed at such an

129 This was occurring—understandably—as the end of the Marshall Plan approached. The "free space" Albert had created for himself shuttling between the Federal Reserve Board and the ECA was about to dissolve, and he, having won the battle . . . feared the consequences. Note that even in the Colombian experience that followed, Hirschman tried, typically, "for liberty's sake," to steer between the World Bank and the Colombian government. The less-than-inspiring affair narrated in "A Dissenter's Confession"—see below, sec. 7—must have convinced him, finally, to set his sights on university teaching. *The Strategy* is also the result of this change in his professional perspective. It is here that he finally achieved his extraordinary success. ("This is Albert in his glory," Sarah Hirschman told me in the early 2000s, showing me a photograph from that happy time).

130 But here again Albert was most likely not "telling the whole story," because, as we know, the end of the Marshall Plan coincided with the rise of McCarthyism. Perhaps he realized that the public career prospects in the U.S. for a democratic and enterprising "wandering Jew" were waning. Perhaps he suspected that the U.S. security apparatus had opened a "file" with his name on it—which actually happened: cf. Adelman (2013, ch. 9).

131 He had written twin essays on international trade that hinted at this interest (Hirschman, 1951, 1952; Meldolesi, 1987, 1995, ch. 1). Moreover, thanks to the recent publication of a July 13, 1951 letter to Manlio Rossi-Doria, I learned that Albert had also considered the possibility of coming to Italy for a year or possibly more (Rossi-Doria, 2011, p. 64 and Meldolesi, 2013, pp. 119–121).

important *causa causans* of his desire to leave his job at the Federal Reserve *ex abrupto*.[132]

(7) There is also a second order of observations concerning the genesis of *The Strategy* that can be made alongside the story just narrated.

Undoubtedly, further exploration of this now-classic volume requires better contextualization by critics, perhaps a multi-angled approach. One possible route is by way of its "Italian" genesis,[133] another is the one just discussed that runs through Washington (and Paris),[134] while a third draws on "how to complicate economics."[135] A fourth would be biographical.[136] But there are certainly others as well. The one we will now briefly seek to focus on suggests a reverse path. Rather than starting with one or more aspects of the author's historical and theoretical background as a gateway to understanding the text, it invokes one of the book's key themes—in our case, the theory of linkages—in order to further examine[137] its theoretical significance in light of the elements enunciated thus far (and to hint finally at its topicality and relevance *chez nous*).

In essence, it is a matter of recognizing that *The Strategy* contains a theoretical breakthrough of the first magnitude in the real sense of the term, arising primarily from the observation[138] of the expansion of Colombia's pulp

132 On the other hand, as mentioned above, we can of course also speculate, with the benefit of hindsight, as to why Hirschman never wanted to publish a selection of his texts from the Marshall Plan era in the United States, and why, until recently, the two most important unpublished ones (see sec. 3 above)—"Proposal" and "Approaches"—appeared only in Italian.

133 Meldolesi (2013, ch. 3).

134 Cf., above, n. 94.

135 Meldolesi (1995, ch. 2).

136 Adelman (2013, ch. 10).

137 On the "singular incomprehension" of *The Strategy* by the economics literature (cf. Meldolesi, 1995, pp. 61–67).

138 From the beginning of his stay in Colombia, the direct observation of the "micro-foundations of economic development" was a key method of Hirschman's work. In addition, in 1954, in *Research Project, Case Studies of Instances of Successful Economic Development in Colombia*, an unpublished project that aimed to "derive some general lessons for developmental policy from circumstances surrounding concrete cases of successful economic development in underdeveloped areas," he set out to "undertake case studies of outstandingly successful business and cooperative ventures in Colombia, centered on 1) Personality and background of founders and managers. 2) Circumstances surrounding major investment and expansion decisions. 3) Principal factors in growth, obstacles encountered, how overcome, competitive aspects. 4) Costs, price policies, role of tariff protection. 5) Role of foreign technical assistance and financial participation. 6) Hiring,

and paper industry.[139] Indeed, working in this sector (including with an entrepreneur whom I was unfortunately not able to meet[140]) Hirschman realized that many investment decisions set in motion a sequence of upstream and downstream linkages, altering the starting conditions and in turn inducing further consequences (for prices, trade, balance of payments, etc.).[141] Generalizing this observation little by little, and studying its theoretical consequences in depth, Albert was able to develop an original idea of economic development,[142]

training, and personnel policies. 7) Maintenance and research policies. 8) Methods of financing" (Box 36, folder 4. Cf., also, Adelman, 2013, pp. 304 and 308).

139 Hirschman himself made this clear to me on more than one occasion. There are, by the way, two large volumes by Albert, entitled *The Market for Paper and Pulp in Colombia* (1956). In fact, "some firms, such as Ebasco, a New York-based paper and box maker interested in expanding to South America to set up a pulp and paper mill, hired Hirschman to evaluate the market." Hirschman and George Kalmanoff (his junior partner) found "a strong and expanding local demand and also noted the opportunity to converge with several local partners, such as the Institute for Industrial Promotion, as well as several firms such as Carton de Colombia and Manuel Carvajal's firm" (Adelman, 2013, p. 312).

140 I allude here to an event that concerns me. In putting together *Alla scoperta del possibile*, 1994 [1995, English tr. *Discovering the Possible*]—I planned, in agreement with Hirschman, a trip funded by the Ford Foundation to five Latin American countries (Argentina, Chile, Brazil, Colombia and Mexico). At a summer meeting in the Italian Alps, Albert mentioned a number of personalities I ought to meet there. Unfortunately, the Colombian paper entrepreneur he had indicated (Manuel Carvajal) was not in Bogotá in the summer of 1990 when Nicoletta Stame and I sought him out.

141 Regarding the origins of linkages, there is, finally, an insightful remark by Albert dating from 1993 (now in 1995, pp. 115–116) regarding Professor Albert Demangeon economic geography lectures, which he had attended at the HEC in his formative years. *The Strategy*, Hirschman declared at Nanterre (on receiving an honorary degree) "was written right after I had lived for almost five years in Colombia [. . .]. In the many discussions I had with that country's policy makers and entrepreneurs, I learned much about the way industrial and infrastructure investment decisions were taken and how they moved up and down the Colombian territory, with its striking topography and distinct development poles [. . .]. Perhaps it was the interaction of the Colombian experience of the fifties with the still live Parisian memories of the thirties that made me hit on the notion of backward and forward linkages as an important force in the dynamics of the development process."

142 "Upon first encountering the frenzy of development," wrote Judith Tendler (1968, p. xi), "the researcher almost naturally backs away from his subject, seeing everything as unrelieved chaos and disorganization. A prior reading of *The Strategy* impels him into the midst of these events with the feeling that, if he is patient enough, he will find a rich complexity of both success and failure, efficiency alongside incompetence, order cohabiting with disorder."

a crucial component of the point of view mentioned earlier that was considerably at odds with current doctrines.[143]

"I originally defined a linkage (or linkages)," he later wrote,[144] "as a characteristic, more or less compelling sequence of investment decisions occurring in the course of industrialization and, more generally, of economic development. In putting forward the concept [. . .] I implicitly criticized the then dominant Harrod-Domar growth model in which growth depends only on the capital-output ratio and on the availability of capital as determined by the propensity to save and the inflow of capital from abroad. More generally, the [linkage] concept arose from a perspective contesting the conventional representation of an economy where natural resources, factors of production, and entrepreneurship are all unequivocally available in given, if scarce, amounts and need only be efficiently allocated to various activities for best results. Instead I contended that 'development depends not so much on finding optimal combinations for given resources and factors of production as on calling forth and enlisting for development purposes resources and abilities that are hidden, scattered, or badly utilized.'[145] This view led me to search for various inducing and mobilizing mechanisms. The resulting 'strategy of unbalanced growth'[146] values investment decisions not only because of their immediate contribution to output, but because of the larger or smaller impulse such decisions are likely to impart to further investment, that is, because of their linkages."[147] Hirschman's treatment, as he wrote to François Perroux in 1959, "arises *wholly* from the need to maximize what I call the induced decision-making process of underdeveloped countries."[148]

143 Note how the very title of the book, *The Strategy of Economic Development*, alludes to the intimate link between analysis and policy, which is characteristic of Hirschman's theoretical work.

144 Hirschman (1989, p. 56).

145 Hirschman (1958, p. 5).

146 This gave rise to a famous controversy because official development economics through some of its most notable representatives (such as Lewis, Nurkse, Rosestein-Rodan, Rostow, Scitovsky), had instead suggested certain classically or neo-classically derived theories of balanced growth.

147 As Hirschman wrote to Chenery in 1959: "I conceive of the ability to invest as a floor and I am most interested in the forces, inducement mechanisms, pressures, pacing devices (these concepts are all more important and recur throughout the book) that permit the economy to develop at a faster rate than would result from the growth of what I define rather restrictively as the 'ability to invest.'"

148 (Cit. in Meldolesi, 1995, p. 236, n. 17).

In contrast to traditional economic thinking, Albert in this way assumes that in the society under consideration there will be a certain level of slack, such that capacities and resources are always available and can be enlisted for development through inducement mechanisms, stratagems, and devices that set the pace (pressures, tensions, cognitive dissonance, etc.). In this way, a condition of under-employment (and, therefore, a low level of productive activity relative to what could be produced), linked to uncertainty about the future, a general feature of economic life,[149] *can* be "headed off" by private, public, and public-private initiatives.[150]

For humankind these are "glad tidings," not least because they clearly suggest that the process of economic growth can be set in motion (or revived) in many ways, and at different levels, by initiatives concerning this or that sector (or group of sectors) of the matrix of the economy, by anyone in a position to schedule and/or inject the corresponding impetus. Such an action (private, public or private-public) can spark a process of economic development and job growth through (at one and the same time) the investment decisions made and their linkage sequences (which within certain limits can be estimated separately, alongside one another). This process will be more robust (with respect to the funding provided), the sounder the investment is (in economic and employment terms), the more significant the "bundles" of linkages are (of production and labor) that correspond to it—and thus the more the investment attracts and enlists available capacities and resources to the productive activity, through mechanisms of inducement and non-equilibrium dynamics.

Of course, this is not the place to delve into the reasoning of *The Strategy*, or to retrace step by step the course of this discovery and the many developments that Hirschman later drew from the linkage effect (upstream and downstream, consumption, fiscal, etc.)[151] To the point, in fact, of generalizing it in

149 Hirschman (1967, ch. 2).

150 This brings to mind what Albert had written in "France and Italy: Patterns of Reconstruction" (Hirschman, 1947a, p. 366): "Economic policy has [. . .] been widely divergent in the two countries. In France parties bitterly opposed to each other in the political field have rallied around the Monnet Plan [. . .]. It may be that the idea of a national economic goal appeals strongly to the French people because of the frustrating lack of direction from which they suffered during the interwar period. Italy, on the contrary, emerged cruelly disillusioned from a long period of excessive 'dynamism,' and the considerable progress achieved in Italian reconstruction has resulted largely from the confluence of individual ventures, with or without encouragement from the State."

151 Cf. Hirschman "A Generalized Linkage Approach to Development, with Special Reference to Staples" (1977a); and "Linkages in Economic Development" (1986b) one of

such a way as to conceive of a country's development as characterized (and, in a sense, generated) by a certain constellation of linkages[152]—that is, by specific drivers of private and public supply-side investment decisions (including, of course, process and product innovation) that complement the driving action of income and demand.[153] I think on the contrary that within the limits of the present exercise, a retrospective clarification of the relationship between this conception and investment planning[154] may help bring the reasoning home to us, and may also point, finally, to some emblematic dilemmas of the present.

(8) In fact, to understand *The Strategy* today with (at least) the intention of putting some of its suggestions into practice, we need in my opinion to guard against spontaneous retrospective anachronism—after so many years of living with a conservative ultra-liberal mindset known to be hostile to any sort of economic planning.

First of all, *chez* Albert things are not that way at all. "The linkage dynamic," he wrote,[155] "made it possible to visualize the industrialization process in terms of an input-output matrix, most of whose cells would be empty to start with, but would progressively fill up in large part because of backward and forward linkage effects. This close connection with Leontief's input-output model, [. . .] contributed to [the linkage model's] favorable reception." But it also suggested (to many) a descriptive interpretation that delegated the interpretation of the

the "entries" written, as mentioned, for *The New Palgrave*, and published as ch. 3 of *Rival Views*.

152 "Taken together, production, consumption, and fiscal linkages [. . .] from the outset [. . .] underscore the existence of very different experiences, of development and underdevelopment paths that correspond to linkage bundles of different staples and of the constellation, force, speed and reliability of linkages that had already been activated. Just as new colors on a painter's palette open up the possibility of a whole range of variations and tonalities, so the evaluation of different combinations of linkages allows us to grasp much of the complexity of development" (Meldolesi, 1995, pp. 84–85).

153 For a contemporary take on the problem of linkages as "A Network View of Development," see Hidalgo and Hausman (2008) and Ginzburg (2012). I think Albert would have appreciated this development. Indeed, I remember the disappointment on his face when I showed him Michael Porter's analysis, which was rather meager on this point.

154 Perhaps linking it later to the other key production line that originated with *The Strategy* and which, as mentioned in ch. 1, ultimately ends up with "how an enterprise manages to endure."

155 Hirschman (1986, p. 58).

development process 'elsewhere' and thus ended up bringing the reasoning back into the (Leontevian) fold of traditional economic theory.[156]

What was lost sight of as a result was the key analytical and normative novelty of *The Strategy*. This had arisen, as mentioned above, from a close observation of the Colombian economic reality and was expressed, for example, in a 1959 letter to André Gunder Frank as follows: "I am in favor of utilizing the energy which holds together economic nuclei of given minimum size in the *building up* of those nuclei"[157]—in other words, fully exploiting for development purposes the inducement mechanisms that link together the economic interrelationships of production, consumption, taxation, etc. Conclusion: the strategy of economic development—this is Albert's thesis—"has important implications for investment planning: it proposes that dynamic considerations, based on the linkages, should be allowed to complement the criterion of static efficiency."[158]

On the other hand, it will be recalled that in the conclusions of *The Strategy*, Albert wrote that "while the choice of priority areas must of course proceed from an examination of the economy as a whole, it may be best, once the choice is made, to concentrate on detailed concrete programs for these areas, as in the first Monnet Plan for France's postwar reconstruction."

Drawing on his extraordinary experience in military and civilian procurement during World War II, Jean Monnet had in the immediate postwar period launched the French plan that bears his name, placing special emphasis on the overall "balance sheet" (i.e., on the responsibility of planning with respect to the national economy as a whole, thus moving beyond the division-of-labor method previously used by individual administrations). He had also stressed the commitment of stakeholders (entrepreneurs, technicians, professionals, trade unionists) from the different sectors involved in the work, as well as some sectors that were considered to be of key importance.[159] This was an approach

156 Typical in this regard was the (largely delusional) discussion on the measurement of linkages. As for the relationship between the sequence of linkages and Wassily Leontief's input-output analysis, it is true that expressing himself in Leontievian terms facilitated the reception of Albert's ideas, but it also encouraged a distorted reading of his work because the crucial diachronic aspect of sequencing was being muted. This is also why historical research has made it possible to capture the development of linkages that could not emerge from the synchronic input-output approach (Hirschman, 1986, p. 58).

157 Hirschman (1986, p. 27).

158 Hirschman (1986, pp. 56–57).

159 Cf. Monnet (1976; English tr. 1977): "Our prime task, undoubtedly," he wrote, for example (p. 246), "was to draw up an overall balance-sheet of France's needs and resources; but unlike some people I did not believe that we should treat all sectors alike. Although we

that was successful, not least because "with France already having its own program for national recovery, it was natural for this mechanism to be utilized when Western Europe as a whole was called upon by the Marshall Plan to establish a joint recovery plan."[160]

Looking at *The Strategy* from this angle makes it clear that a proper grasp of this text requires the prior reading of two short "Colombian" papers of Albert's (later included in Hirschman, 1971)[161] that deal specifically with planning, promoting the in-depth study of certain sectors and suggesting that alongside specific plans, there should be a "search for a body of principles and meaningful generalizations which would permit the economist to be concretely helpful in the location and elaboration of promising, specific investment projects."[162]

set up a total of eighteen Modernization Commissions, all of the same type, this was to enable us to form a complete and consistent picture. When the time came to act, I knew that we should have to concentrate on five or six decisive points." In addition, just before this (p. 235), he had written: "The question was: where to begin? Once again, I realized that this was *the only question that mattered*. Once you have made a start, all you need to do is continue" (emphasis added). As we can see, here again it is, in the words of the later Hirschman (see below in this chapter), a matter of finding the most appropriate mix of simultaneity and sequence.

160 Hirschman (1998, p. 34). "The Monnet Plan is the result of a cooperative effort on the part of French Government, industry and labor. It does not detail a rigid program for every branch of economic activity for the next four years, but rather sets goals for such aggregate magnitudes as national income, investment, labor force, and required foreign aid. It provides specifically, however, for considerable expansion and modernization of the French internal transportation system and of coal, electricity, steel, cement, and agricultural machinery. With the exception of the last of these, the branches of industry toward which the main effort of the Plan is to be directed are either nationalized or highly concentrated."

161 I refer here to "Economics and Investment Planning: Reflections Based on Experience in Colombia" (1954a) and "Economic Policy in Underdeveloped Countries" (1957), now in Hirschman, *A Bias for Hope. Essays on Development and Latin America* (1971). (This is the book Albert alludes to at the end of "Fifty Years After the Marshall Plan," when he writes: "some of the key notions of my later writings on development, such as a 'Passion for the Possible' and a 'Bias for Hope,' may go back to Marjolin's concept of 'an apparently absurd, but successful wager,' which for him was a principal characteristic of the Marshall" (Hirschman, 1998, p. 43).

162 Hirschman (1971, p. 44). Albert argues that from the simple observation that these countries generally suffer from inadequate maintenance of capital, one can derive the criterion that priority should be given to investments that either need almost no maintenance or must necessarily have maintenance that is stipulated. In addition, it should be noted that industries that are potential buyers of the country's agricultural products initially import such products and only then source them domestically. After that, as a result of

Emphasizing experimentation and improvisation, these papers also begin to examine policy making.

So, if we take this route, *The Strategy* begins to look like what it actually is. That is to say, a text that offers an economic development strategy based on thinking which is "collateral" to the construction of the plan while still compatible with investment and employment planning, and whose purpose is to vigorously reinforce public intervention. Indeed, it aims to consciously direct such intervention so as to make it significantly more effective/efficient.

This view also lends a different meaning to Albert's well-known dispute with the World Bank on planning as told in "A Dissenter's Confession." It is true that Hirschman refused to draft a plan for Colombia based on (somewhat senseless) dictates from the Bank and chose instead to investigate why, as a local functionary put it, *aqui al tropico hacemos todo al réves*. But this should certainly not be read as hostility toward planning as such.

Rather, it was a rebellion against a specific planning procedure imposed by the Bank[163] which, because of the Pindaric leap it entailed (supported, incidentally, by a very influential segment of the economics discipline), and also because of the crippled state of Colombian statistics, in fact flew in the face of common sense.

Conclusion—planning, certainly, but with feet on the ground, while at the same time compensating for the many difficulties with an unprecedented

their "release" into the market, these domestic products become standardized. "These observations," as I commented at the time (Meldolesi, 1995, p. 48) "seem episodic. But in fact they are decisive 'findings' that later evolve into key propositions." The first concerns the degree of tolerance for poor performance, from which flows line of thinking concerning "how an enterprise manages to endure" (which also includes the exit-voice relationship). The second has to do with the upstream connections that finally flow into the "production line" of "one thing leading (or not leading) to another."

163 It was believed at the time, as Hirschman explained in "A Dissenter's Confession" (1984, p. 8), that there was already "adequate knowledge without close study of local surroundings, of the likely ranges of savings and capital-output ratios, and those estimates, joined to the country's latest national income and balance of payments accounts, would yield all the key figures needed to indicate how much foreign capital would be required to achieve the desired rate of increase in national income per capita." As Albert had written 30 years before (1954; now in 1971, pp. 46–47), if the economist devotes his skills "primarily to the elaboration of comprehensive investment programs projecting everything ten or more years ahead, he runs the risk of bringing about, in the economic sphere, a counterpart to a state of affairs which André Siegfried found characteristic, some twenty years ago, of political life in many Latin American countries: the contrast between fine theory and wretched practice."

complementary strategy. This is the basic economic policy choice underlying *The Strategy*. And it seems to me that this is precisely how it can (and should) continue to be used in any well-defined territory (municipality, region, country) as an indispensable addition to a well-constructed project (or plan).

(9) As we know, when his biennial contract ran out (April 1954), the situation created in Colombia after the coup led by General Rojas Pinilla, Hirschman "set up shop" in Bogotá as a private consultant.[164] This is undoubtedly another key experience in the genesis of *The Strategy*. Indeed, while supporting and developing planning, the book hinges on the search for hidden rationales and the elucidation of immediate experience—which comes from observing the behavior of private sector as well as public sector insiders (even, within limits, with their own cooperation).[165]

I have pointed out elsewhere[166] that there are numerous similarities and correspondences between Albert Hirschman's Marshall Plan texts and the "Colombian" texts—an indication that this way of thinking (moving outside the deductivist purview of standard economics in order to instead interact with reality), inaugurated successfully in Washington and in Europe,[167] found in the end (even more) fertile ground in Colombia.

I would now like to try out another exercise, more suited to the other side of the fence—the world of practical, operational people (since beyond examining texts in detail, it seems to me instructive to discuss a concrete situation involving *The Strategy*). In fact, to truly appreciate this the reader would in my opinion have to engage with this "strategy" from the vantage point of his or her own private and/or public intervention experience—which is not easy for a number of reasons. First of all, it would require an ability to think *mutatis mutandis* (i.e., adapting the book to one's own reality, in general quite different

164 And enjoyed immediate success. Even to the point that an entrepreneur whom Nicoletta Stame and I met at the Industrial Union of Bogotá in 1990 (when I was preparing my *Discovering the Possible*) was very surprised to learn from us that Albert had had a technical career as an economist in the public sector and had then embarked on a university career—with great success.

165 In the preface to *The Strategy* (1958) Albert declared that he took great encouragement, when he began planning the book, from the following passage from Whitehead (1930, p. 6): "The elucidation of immediate experience is the sole justification of any thought; and the starting point for thought is the analytic observation of components of this experience."

166 Cf. the texts cit. above in n. 101.

167 Cf. Asso and de Cecco (1987) and the texts cit. in n. 101.

from the context Hirschman studied), because today we find ourselves in a different era, one in which the dominant culture in economics is not friend of planning, and because dirtying their hands with these dormant things will not be everyone's cup of tea.

Therefore, for didactic purposes, and *pour encourager les autres*, I will try and recall schematically some aspects of a small planning experience that I set up with Marco Vitale.[168] Briefly, some fixed points of similarity with those encountered above (sec. 8) can be drawn from a trip Vitale made to Campania, which I recounted in *Milano-Napoli* (2010), as well as from the work we developed together at the Industrial Union of Naples, and finally from the candidacy of Umberto Ambrosoli for the presidency of the Lombardy Region.

The point is, suppose we ourselves take general (not sectoral) responsibility for development and employment in a certain area, and suppose further that we build up some reasonable ideas about this with the help of technicians, professionals, entrepreneurs, union leaders, etc. who are experts in the fields discussed—like cities of cities, specific territorial projects, employment goals linked (directly and indirectly) to possible investments, financial, administrative, and organizational aspects of the project, etc. And suppose finally that in the process we manage to establish some priorities for production, employment, and internationalization. The key question then becomes: with all this in mind, can we turn at this point to *The Strategy* in order to, in a sense, renew our momentum ("find an extra gear") on top of what we have already constructed?

The answer in my view is yes, for the following reasons. In the first place, the analysis of linkages can significantly improve (or orient or strengthen) the investment program we have set in motion. Second, there are times when "putting the cart before the horse" in a development sequence can raise productivity per euro (and per person). Third, the idea of an "optimal imbalance" in economic growth[169] is useful in the retrieval (and enlistment for development) of capacities and resources that are hidden, dispersed, or badly utilized. Furthermore, a moderate increase in prices (and/or in the population) can favor development. It is also the case that, through investments in machinery with a narrow margin for poor performance, a certain industrial rhythm can be imposed *sic et simpliciter* on the work, and this rhythm, through spontaneous contagion (and some ad hoc arrangements) can be "exported" within the relevant territory—in the private sector as well as the public. And finally, because

168 Vitale (2008); Meldolesi (2010b); Vitale (2013).

169 Hirschman and Lindblom (1962); Hirschman (1971, 1986); Meldolesi (1994a).

in this regard, Hirschman shows later[170] that there is also another side to the coin, etc.

"In spite of its title and of its origin in practical advisory work in Colombia, *The Strategy* [. . .]," Albert wrote,[171] "was widely regarded as a contribution to development theory. A simple principle—'unbalanced growth' or the idea of maximizing induced decision making—was here shown to yield suggestions on a wide range of development problems, from investment priorities to industrialization patterns,[172] from inflation and balance-of-payments policies to new attitudes toward population growth, from the choice of technology to the role of the state in development."

We may conclude that for any program for a specific territorial context, the best we have been able to devise, there is indeed a second "dossier" by means of which the first one can be significantly improved—namely the economic development strategy left to us by Albert Hirschman. It is by this means, in fact, that in a certain sense our projects are able to stand on their own two feet instead of just one.

"Against 'one thing at a time'"

(10) As we know, the viewpoint indicated above was later complemented and further developed in *Journeys Toward Progress* (1963) and *Development Projects Observed* (1967) books that deal with certain development problems from the standpoint of, respectively, decision-making and administration. Along with *The Strategy*, they make up a trilogy that aims to celebrate the epic tale of development.[173] In my view, however, they also point to a general art of conversation

170 Hirschman (1967).

171 Hirschman (1995, p. 86).

172 "Following Gerschenkron," Hirschman later recalled (1986, p. 15), "I saw originality and creativity in deviating from the path followed by the older industrial countries, in skipping stages, and in inventing sequences that had a 'wrong way around' look. It was surely this attitude that permitted me to ferret out the backward and forward linkage dynamic and to acclaim as a dialectical-paradoxical feat what was later called, with disparaging intent, import-substituting industrialization."

173 "The three books were of course conceived consecutively. The concept—or fantasy—of a unified 'trilogy' emerged in my mind primarily during the writing of the third book. Over and above the overt purpose of my work—the analysis of development and the advice on policy—I came to see it as having the latent, hidden, but overriding common intent and function: to celebrate, to 'sing' the epic adventure of development—its challenge, drama, and grandeur" (Hirschman, 1995, p. 128).

among different points of view (of technicians, politicians, officials) in order to gradually, and in the best way possible, master a complex reality such as our own societies, for the purpose of development (that is, the development of democracy and social justice).

With this in mind, I now come to an episode that I witnessed which concerns *The Strategy*, and with economics as a starting point, begins a dialogue with politics. I spoke of it earlier, actually.[174] Those first days in November 1989 when the Berlin Wall came down were a watershed, not least from the standpoint of Hirschmanian self-subversion. To properly grasp this, it is not enough just to remember that auspicious turning point. We must look to a talk from those days entitled "The Case Against 'One Thing at a Time,'" and originally presented at the University of Buenos Aires when the author was awarded an honorary degree at a conference (organized by the Inter-American Development Bank at the Di Tella Institute) on the topic "Hirschman's Work and a New Development Strategy for Latin America."[175]

"It often happens to the dissenter," Hirschman stated (in a self-deprecating key),[176] "that his or her views become in turn a new orthodoxy. So far this fate has fortunately not befallen *The Strategy of Economic Development*, a book I wrote over thirty years ago as a dissent from prevailing opinions and doctrines. But the occasion for this essay, a conference organized in part to celebrate the old book, may be an ominous cloud on the horizon. I shall therefore use this opportunity to [. . .] present an argument that contradicts or qualifies a central proposition of the book. To be more specific, I intend to show that the validity of that proposition has limits, that it is more applicable in some situations than in others, and finally, that the course I advocated is not without some problems of its own."

Thus, through Hirschman's quiet voice, I encountered for the first time his (then) very new self-subversive propensity—his tendency, that is, to reconsider this or that aspect of his scientific elaboration—almost to the point of double-checking every link—in order to improve its "tightness" (specific and general, current and future) in the face of successive events.

174 Cf., above, ch. 1 n. 19.

175 Hirschman (1995, p. 69). If we begin with the reservations expressed in ch. 6 of *The Strategy* and pass through a well-known 1968 essay entitled "The Political Economy of Import-Substituting Industrialization in Latin America," it is possible to get an idea (however partial) of the logical process which, in parallel with his work on *The Rhetoric*, finally led Albert to this reconsideration (see, in this regard, Meldolesi, 1995, pp. 73–77).

176 Now in Hirschman (1995, p. 69).

It was, in essence, an exercise in toughening the theoretical structure and making it more flexible so that it corresponded as closely as possible to "the way things actually are"—the sort of task that precisely in that period was gaining systematicity and style,[177] and which sprang from a key proposition in *The Strategy* (and the entire Hirschmanian structure)—the sequence of linkages that flows from unbalanced growth.

In *The Strategy*, Albert had argued that "it may be possible and in certain circumstances even desirable to push ahead with, say, industrial development in spite of inadequate infrastructure such as electric power-generating capacity and transportation. I took a positive view of these *kinds* of disequilibria," he affirmed,[178] "because they seemed to me to be self-correcting [. . .] because of the predictable [. . .] reactions on the part of both market forces and public policy responses. But it was far from clear how such corrective forces can be activated when a disequilibrium or disproportionality arises, not between sectors of the economy, but between economic and political progress." Hence the need to narrow and qualify that proposition *post festum*.

Hirschman recalled having been initially taken aback in a conversation in the late 1960s, shortly after the Ongania coup in Argentina, with an official and/or supporter of the new regime, according to whom the regime had decided to follow a sequence of unbalanced growth. "First we must straighten out the economic problems [. . .]; thereafter, we will look out for greater social equity; and only then will the country be ready for a restoration of civil liberties and for other political advances." "I was appalled by this suggestion," Albert declared.[179] "My writings were invoked to justify the 'temporary' suppression or restriction of democratic rights and liberties." It was out of this incident, traveling along intellectual paths that we can only guess at in part, that his clarifying correction finally sprouted 20 years later.

"Considerable economic growth and progress and perhaps also an improvement in the distribution of income can take place without any concomitant

177 Reworking published books to prepare subsequent editions was not "like Hirschman." It is true that he always took special care to ensure that his books, slim and juicy as they are, did not end up out of print. But, in reprintings, the texts always remained unchanged—for any clarifications, additions, qualifications or modifications, Albert used the Preface to the new edition, or additional papers (later published in collections of essays). What changed, however, in the last phase of his scholarly output, was the intent. In fact, this process of rectification and adjustment became deliberate, explicit: it became theoretically necessary.

178 Hirschman (1995, p. 70; original emphasis).

179 *Ibid.*

advance in political openness or decline in repression, just as the inverse development can go on for a considerable period: a strengthening of democracy can go hand in hand with a weakening of the economy. There is no *general* reason why these various good things should necessarily go together except for the fact that we wish it were so—it would make for a less complicated world."[180]

(11) "One can obviously think of some reasons," Albert argues,[181] "why such disequlibria or disproportionalities should bring equilibrating forces into play; but there are others that make for the opposite movement [. . .]. For example, once an authoritarian regime achieves economic progress, the government could very well find itself more popular [. . .] and therefore under less pressure than before to evolve in the direction of pluralism and human rights. Accordingly, one might suspect the good faith of such a government when it says the 'time is not ripe' for moving in this direction [. . .]. There is much commonsense appeal in the old rule 'one thing at a time,' but apparently it can be a mixed blessing to be able to order tasks in this manner." Hence the title (and *leitmotif*) of this important speech.

The argument connects at this point to *The Rhetoric* (1991), the monograph that Hirschman was writing just at that time, and in particular to the reactionary jeopardy thesis, according to which "a step forward *will jeopardize* an earlier progressive step that is to be valued more highly than the one under discussion. The thesis has been put forward primarily in countries like England, which had a long history of *gradual* political and social change."[182]

But what happens to those who don't have such a history behind them? Is it not the case, as the literature on "political development" has long argued, that "in Western Europe, as various authors have pointed out, the distinct 'tasks' of nation building—achieving territorial identity, securing authority all over that territory, enlisting and managing mass participation—were undertaken one after the other, over a period of centuries, while the new nations of the Third World are faced with all of them at once"?[183]

"Let us accept this argument for the moment," Albert argues.[184] "The latecoming countries are then seen to have at least one *advantage* on their side: when they come to adopt, for instance, welfare state institutions, it will

180 *Ibid.*; original emphasis.
181 *Ibid.*, p. 71.
182 *Ibid.*, pp. 71–72; original emphasis.
183 *Ibid.*
184 *Ibid.*, pp. 72–73; original emphasis.

not be possible to combat this advance in the name of preserving a tradition of democracy or of individual liberties since that tradition hardly exists. [. . .] The rhetorical advantage [. . .] may seem a small consolation in comparison to the disadvantage—the need to solve several problems of state building at once [. . .]. But that disadvantage looks rather less formidable," Hirschman affirms at this point (and he looked visibly satisfied reading this passage), "once the underlying argument is called into question."

"To begin with, it is simply not true that the advanced countries always enjoy the luxury of sequential problem solving, whereas latecomers are uniformly forced into a virtually simultaneous operation. [. . .]. Take the stages of industrialization: [. . .] the latecomers, for a change, are the ones able to move leisurely, in accordance with the backward linkage dynamic, from the last stages of production to the earlier ones [. . .] while the pioneering industrial countries often had to produce concurrently all needed inputs." But this, Hirschman continues, "has been considered an *advantage* (from the point of view of the dynamic of industrialization), whereas the sequential nature of the industrialization process among the later industrializers could be looked at correspondingly as a drawback, because of the risks of getting stuck at the finished consumer goods stage."[185]

In conclusion, he points out that "a comparison of the dynamics of industrialization and of political development seems to yield at first only one rather disconcerting generalization: no matter whether the tasks facing the advanced countries can be tackled sequentially or must be solved all at once, these countries always have the better part of the deal."[186]

(12) But he doesn't stop here. "Actually, there is a more interesting conclusion to be drawn from the comparison of the two dynamics: leisurely, sequential problem-solving is not necessarily a pure blessing, as has been so plausibly argued in the literature on political development"—which, as mentioned, Hirschman was examining in depth while writing *The Rhetoric*. He argues[187]

185 *Ibid.*, p. 73; original emphasis. This is an important point in *The Strategy*, which states: "The industrialist who has worked hitherto with imported materials will often be hostile to the establishment of domestic industries producing these materials." More generally: "Whereas the first steps are easy to take by themselves, they can make it difficult to take the next ones" (Hirschman, 1958, pp. 118–119).

186 Hirschman (1995, pp. 73–74). "But that should come as no surprise," the passage continues. "it is one of the interlocking reasons why these countries *are* advanced."

187 *Ibidem*; original emphasis. Hirschman refers here to the section "When One Thing Forestalls Another; Mapping the Getting Stuck Syndrome" from the essay "The Rhetoric of Reaction—Two Years Later" (1993; now in 1995, ch. 2).

that in fact, "*sequential problem-solving brings with it the risk of getting stuck*. This risk may apply not only to the sequence from the production of consumer goods to that of machinery and intermediate goods, but, in a different form, to the complex progression sketched in a famous 1949 lecture by the English sociologist T. H. Marshall" (which, by the way, Albert uses to start off the reasoning of *The Rhetoric*).

"A society which has pioneered in securing these [individual] liberties," Hirschman adds, thinking in all likelihood of the U.S. under Reagan and of Mrs. Thatcher's Britain,[188] "is likely to experience special difficulties in subsequently establishing comprehensive social welfare policies. The very values that serve such a society well in one phase—the belief in the supreme value of individuality, the insistence on individual achievement and individual responsibility—may be something of an embarrassment later on when a communitarian, solidaristic ethos needs to be stressed."

"Perhaps this is the basic explanation why social welfare policies were pioneered by Bismarck's Germany, a country singularly unencumbered by a strong liberal tradition. Similarly, the recent rhetorical assault against the welfare state in the West has not been nearly as vigorous and sustained in Continental Western Europe as in England and the United States. None of this implies that in countries with a strong liberal tradition it is impossible to establish a comprehensive set of social welfare policies. But it is here that their introduction appears to require the concurrence of exceptional circumstances, such as the pressures created by depression or war, as well as special feats of social, political, and ideological engineering."[189]

(13) This brings us to the heart of the matter. "The argument I have just developed," Albert states,[190] "is in many ways the exact counterpoint to my argument in favor of unbalanced growth of more than thirty years ago. In *The Strategy* I argued against the idea that, because of the interdependence of the economy from either the supply or the demand side, no progress could be achieved unless

188 Hirschman (1995, p. 74). Cf. Hirschman (1982a; now in 1986, ch. 5, 1985, 1991, 2013, ch. 4).

189 Hirschman (1995, p. 74). Probably, the allusion is to the retrospective evaluations of the Roosevelt era cited in the previous note. "Moreover," the passage continues, "once introduced, welfare state provisions will again come under attack at the first opportunity. The tension between the liberal tradition and the new solidarity ethos will remain unresolved for a long time, and the jeopardy thesis will be invoked with predictable regularity and will always find a receptive audience."

190 *Ibid*.

expansion of investment and output were increased simultaneously in all key sectors by means of 'integrated investment planning,' or a 'big push.'[191] Instead, I searched, in theory as well as in actual historical development experiences, for the possibility of *sequential* solutions to the growth problem."

"But now my argument has come full circle," he continues,[192] "as I have met with some real drawbacks of sequential solutions, particularly where interdependence among tasks is weak or nonexistent. The problem may then be the opposite: several tasks need to be undertaken, but far from requiring an 'integrated' approach and solution as a result of interdependence, they are all too separable. In such circumstances, it is easy and tempting to move forward in only one of several desirable policy areas, with the idea or pretext that others are going to be tackled later on. But [. . .] that first advance may make it more difficult and perhaps impossible to act later in the other areas."

"In closing, let me plead that the intellectual path I have followed is not altogether bizarre. Repelled by a policy prescription,[193] I elaborated an alternative approach. Later I looked at some situations where events had taken the sequential course and noticed that it in turn harbored some dangers and risks of its own. This is only natural, for there is no riskless action."[194]

"Rather, the story I have told here has two lessons. First, there is a compensation or, to go back to a favorite concept of mine [from *The Strategy* on], a blessing in disguise in store for those societies which come up all at once against a variety of policy tasks other countries were able to solve one after the other over a very long period.[195] Second, looking for uniform solutions to development problems invariably leads us astray; this is so for the imperatives

191 The reference to balanced growth theory here is to Rosenstein-Rodan and Nurkse on the demand side, and to Scitovsky and Lewis on the supply side: Hirschman (1958, ch. 3, n. 1). See also sec. 7 and n. 146 above.

192 Hirschman (1995, p. 75). "It often is the case, of course," the author continues, "that politicians who use the 'one thing at a time' or the 'time is not ripe' arguments are not really eager to move in those areas of public policy or reform that they say they must 'unfortunately' postpone."

193 *Ibid.*, p. 76. Because it "seemed to me excessively demanding, dangerous in its policy implications, as well as simply wrong."

194 "Recognizing those risks," Albert points out (*ibid.*), "does not mean either that we should not act at all or that the proposition against which I argued originally is rehabilitated."

195 This is a proposition, by the way, that Italy should also face up to, considering the numerous economic, political and administrative "hiccups" (shall we say) that have piled up over time and have gone hand in hand with the prevailing tendency of least resistance—a "live and let live" attitude that must instead be overcome. Because—and this is the moral of the story—if we want to, we can.

of simultaneity and sequentiality alike, that is, for the insistence on 'integrated planning' as well as for the injunction to postpone certain tasks in the name of 'one thing at a time.'"[196]

What emerges here is a mature, pragmatic attitude, able to guard against both dangers, and at the same time to identify the most promising way forward in a mix of simultaneity and sequentiality that is tailored to the concrete situation—something undeniably "built in" in Hirschman's attitude since the days of the Marshall Plan.

"With this conclusion," Albert declares in bidding farewell, "I can lay claim to at least one element of continuity in my thought: the refusal to define 'one best way.'"[197]

A Few Concluding Words

All well and good—the reader might think at this point. But have we properly grasped the key message in this argument? What does it suggest for our own daily lives?

Perhaps the simplest way to try and answer this is to mirror Albert's analytical and normative discourse in our current "predicaments"—keeping our own situation in mind along with his intentions and suggestions—and perhaps benefiting (in very simple and somewhat allusive form) from what some friends and/or fellow economists have written on the subject. Shortly before his passing, a friend of Hirschman's (and mine) who died prematurely, Tommaso Padoa-Schioppa, argued in a brief memorandum addressed to the Greek government that an expansionary policy of the kind the Euro-zone needs can only be pursued at the European level, simply because macroeconomic management of the economy presupposes the full sovereignty that the Euro countries have (partly, but more than the other countries in the community) transferred to the central level. Therefore, our countries must "adapt," willingly or otherwise, to the macroeconomic conditions decided at that higher level. And as two old friends now demised (Fernando Vianello and Andrea Ginzburg) had rightly argued, the Germany that dominated at the time the European scene (including the Euro-zone and the EU institutions) had been pursuing a policy of low growth and budgetary austerity, with the dismal consequences we all knew.[198]

196 Hirschman (1995, p. 76).

197 *Ibid.*

198 Vianello (2013) and Ginzburg (2012).

Fortunately, however, this was not the whole story—we also needed to see the underlying blessing paradoxically hiding in this situation. Actually, if nothing else, the theoretical and practical rediscovery of the lesson of *The Strategy* at all levels—private, public-private, public (municipal, regional, national)—could have affectively softened out our agony.[199]

The fact is, Albert's reasoning *can* be generalized, his perspective *can* become a tool of conscious action for a myriad of development actors along with those who support and surround them.

The point is, it is up to *everyone* (entrepreneurs, professionals, technicians, managers, teachers, administrators, politicians, citizens) to act directly and/or indirectly to ensure that the enormous potentials are properly tapped. All management activities can be mobilized and steered toward promoting (and supporting) development by coupling projects with Hirschmanian strategies.

Italians, for instance, tired of waiting, *can* take back an important share of the functions of development. They can transform the country—its economy, its state, cultural and social system—making it more active and more effective/efficient. A revival of this kind, undoubtedly within our grasp, would enable us to have more of a voice internationally, not least in Brussels.[200]

199 In other words, no one who actually understands the issue can get out of it by claiming that it is not up to him.

200 This is how I see it, and showing that this is indeed possible has been an explicit (and, for an individual project, well-founded) ambition of my long teaching career in Naples. Liliana Baculo, Nicoletta Stame and I, along with many students, have collectively and individually put these ideas into practice. However, experience has also taught us that it is not enough to attain a certain leadership role in one's own environment. Once the boundaries of one's own responsibilities have been crossed (as a teacher, entrepreneur, manager, technician, or student) in moving toward a proposed course of action involving a section of the public system, if you are not wholly independent, it is also imperative to reach a political agreement with those in charge (which is far from easy). But this is still not enough. Administrative conditions that allow the measure to be put into practice are also indispensable—a change in the way things actually work, that is, so as to bring it about.

· 3 ·

ON THE POLITICAL LEGACY

(1) Certain propositions that were first put forward in the two "Colombian" articles in 1954 and 1957[201] and later developed in *The Strategy* became so important in Hirschman's overall body of work that I was able to point to them, with his consent, as the *cardo* and *decumanus* of the Hirschmanian *polis* (or, in Bogotá, the *calle* and the *carrera*—as Albert added on the same occasion, with a hint of self-irony).[202]

I am referring, of course, to linkages and latitude for poor performance, which, over time, have evolved and finally been renamed respectively "one thing leading (or not leading) to another," and "how an enterprise manages to endure." I do not intend to return to the complex history of their construction, branching and development during which our author gradually built up a broad array of possibilities for studying economic, political and economic-political (and more) relations. I would like to show instead that some aspects of them (in addition to the ones we looked at in the two

201 Cf., above, ch. 2., sec. 8 and n. 162.

202 And revealing, however, that he was less than well versed in Roman history . . . Cf. Meldolesi (1995, p. 161).

preceding chapters) were additionally and significantly corrected by Albert in his last formulation.[203]

First of all, let us look again at the unbalanced growth sequence which, as we have just seen, emerged initially from an intersectoral economic analysis and was then applied in economics and politics. As noted, it appears in "A Dissenter's Confession" (1984) in the form of a "tacking" route against the wind, whereby advancing on one side of the relationship requires a lesser degree of retreat on the other.

A sequence of this nature appears once again in *A Propensity to Self-Subversion* in the essay "The On and Off Connection between Political and Economic Progress"[204] as a way of exploring further relationships particular to economics and politics. Here Hirschman briefly recalls some relationships that he considers standard in economics and politics (all good things go together, one thing jeopardizes another or vice versa, advancement on one side requires a temporary sacrifice on the other—renamed "*per aspera ad astra*" ["through hardship to the stars"][205])—for the purpose of introducing still more interrelations under the heading "From Economics to Politics: The Ratchet Effect and Related Metaphors" and "From Political to Economic Progress: Toward a Repertoire of History's Tricks."

"What, then, is the point of my story?"—that Albert[206] left behind. "It is to affirm once again that political and economic progress are not tied together in any easy, straightforward, functional way. There are the various on-and-off connections" evoked above. "Then there are stories, intricate and often nonrepeatable [. . .] that look more like tricks history has up its sleeve than like social-scientific regularities, not to speak of laws. To make an inventory, to survey history's repertoire of such tricks, seems to me an appropriately modest way of trying to make progress with this difficult topic."

203 *Ibid.*, ch. 3 and 6. I refer of course to the "voice-exit" qualifications in ch. 1 regarding "how an enterprise manages to endure" on one side, and on the other those aspects "against 'one thing at a time'" from ch. 2 that concern "why one thing leads (or doesn't lead) to another."

204 Written originally in German in 1990–1991, it was published (in German and English) in 1992; now in Hirschman (1995, ch. 19).

205 Even though among Albert's papers the exact opposite is also to be found—that is *per aspera ad disastra*, the motto of the 4w club (where we went wrong) that Hirschman founded for fun at Harvard in 1972 (box 54, folder 4).

206 Hirschman (1995, p. 229).

The Self-Subversion of Shifting Involvements

(2) Thus, having taken on board the criticism of "one thing at a time,"[207] re-examining the sequential relation of economics and politics only requires, as far as we can tell, a further broadening of the spectrum of possibilities.[208] The same is not true, however, for an adjacent field—that of private-public oscillations and interactions.[209]

I am referring in particular to "Melding the Public and the Private Spheres: Taking Commensality Seriously,"[210] an important essay that opens *Crossing Boundaries* (1998), Albert's last collection.[211] "I hope," he explains in no uncertain terms,[212] "to subvert here a book I published in 1982, *Shifting Involvements: Private Interests and Public Action*. It explored the reasons

207 Cf., above, sec. 9–13 of ch. 2.

208 And this is in all likelihood why, in the collection A *Propensity* (1995) it is included, as ch. 19, in the part devoted to "New Forays," and not in the first part: "On Self-Subversion." A similar process probably applies to *The Passions*. In a note in his papers, Albert asks himself why *The Passions* does not need self-subversion—a question that may seem paradoxical or even provocative, mentally accustomed as we are to the inverse relationship—seeing the products of thought as final achievements (see, in this regard, the examples of resistance to self-subversion listed in 1995, p. 91). The answer, from the new preface to *The Passions* (1996), is simply that there is no need for it. It strikes me, however, that there is another possibility. More than self-subversion, perhaps what was needed was a supplement, like Hirschman's review of *The Market Experience*, a "monumental" book by Robert Lane, which appears as ch. 18 ("New Forays") of A *Propensity*. Undoubtedly, in the overall scheme of Albert's work, such a vigorous excursus of market *criticism* "rebalances," in a sense, the "doux commerce" thesis (a propensity he had indeed already displayed in *Rival Views* [1986, ch. 5], where this eighteenth-century thesis was juxtaposed with the opposing thesis of destruction). As if to say that *The Passions*, in and of itself, does not need self-subversion, but my thinking does.

209 Cf., above, sec. 11, ch. 1.

210 Originally presented as the Jan Patocka Memorial Lecture at the Institute of Human Sciences in Vienna in 1996.

211 In addition to the brief excursus on his life that he had already published in Italian under the title *Passaggi di frontiera* (1994), this 1998 book includes only the essay we are about to discuss and "Fifty Years After the Marshall Plan: Two Posthumous Memoirs and Some Personal Recollections" (see above, ch. 2). These last two papers can thus be seen as responding to his extreme desire for analysis, clarification and self-subversion. (That they are the very issues I myself had grappled most with at the time is, personally, a pleasant retrospective surprise. It is here, then, that Albert felt the need to leave us his final "messages in a bottle," and it is these in fact that—at the beginning of the previous chapter and throughout this one—I intend to discuss.)

212 Hirschman (1998, p. 11).

modern societies may be 'predisposed toward oscillation between periods of intense preoccupation with public issues and of almost total concentration on individual improvement and private welfare goals.' Many of the reasons I gave for such periodic shifts seem to me to be valid still. But I want to go back to one particular phase of the alleged 'private/public cycle,' which I now see in a very different light."

"The principal motive force that drove my story was *disappointment.*[213] Disappointment with the concentration on private consumption was for me a primary source of the subsequent turn toward action in the public interest, just as in the following phase disappointment with the turn toward action in the public interest would promote the return to private concerns. It so happened that during the post-World War II period with which I started my account, private consumption in the Western economies rose primarily in the area of durable goods—automobiles, refrigerators, washing machines, televisions, and so on. This 'drive to high mass consumption' was celebrated by Walt W. Rostow in his highly successful work Stages of *Economic Growth* (1960). I wrote my book some twenty years later, with the benefit of hindsight, that is, after the world had passed through the violent student agitation and unrest of the late 1960s, which were widely interpreted as a protest against the latest Rostovian stage. By then that stage had come to be known as 'consumerism,' a term that was often used in a derogatory vein."

Here we can already sense one of the "roots" of *Shifting Involvements.* Albert is reacting (finally, after many years[214]) to the youth uprising of the 1960s,[215] broadening the perspective of the analysis to the entire postwar

213 *Ibid.*, pp. 11–12. "While a life filled with disappointment is a sad affair," he explained in *Shifting Involvements* (1982, p. 23) "a life without any disappointment may not be bearable at all. For disappointment is the natural counterpart of man's propensity to entertain magnificent vistas and aspirations."

214 He was struck by the fact that in Paris in June 1978 many commentators celebrated the tenth anniversary of the events of May 1968. Even while noting that the political enthusiasm that had captured half the world already seemed remote, they simply registered the great change in climate that had occurred. It is a common observation, in fact, that a key ingredient of the "spirit of '68" was a sudden and overwhelming concern for the public interest—for peace, egalitarianism, political participation. But by then, during the 1970s, people had gone back to their private concerns (Hirschman, 1982, p. 3).

215 However, according to the testimony of his son-in-law Alain Salomon (in Vv.Aa., 2013, p. 18), when he and Albert's daughter Katia participated in the student movement at Columbia University in New York in 1968, occupying the architecture department and joining activist groups promoting grassroots projects in the city, Albert's attitude was (to say the least) ambivalent. "Albert was supportive, but had mixed feelings about some of the students' revolutionary pronouncements and tactics. He would listen to my

period and taking the delusion of durable consumption as the central issue. This was the very consumption celebrated by W.W. Rostow in a book whose key idea Hirschman,[216] in the footsteps of Alexander Gerschenkron, criticized bitterly—the idea of stages through which economic development had passed (and so presumably would pass, now and forever).

(3) On the other hand, Rostow is not even mentioned in *Shifting Involvements*, perhaps out of good manners (somewhat elitist, to be honest), or because at the time, Rostow's celebration of the "push toward high mass consumption" was so well-known—even to the uninformed reader—that Albert was able to take it for granted. Therefore, since he had now clarified this aspect of the question, it seems logical to surmise that the desire to "correct" this (apologetic) sort of celebration of consumption was one of the main original sources of *Shifting Involvements*.[217] "Had Rostow been overenthusiastic," the latter-day

ideological demonstrations with great patience and perceptible perplexity. I would show him Situationist texts by Guy Debord and Raoul Vaneigem; he would glance at them murmuring 'I see. . .I see. . ..' I think the student movement appeared to him somewhat immature. We were a voice, but a voice with insufficient quality." As much as it may have been justified in the specific case recalled by Salomon, this attitude of "sufficiency" (not to say aristocratic paternalism) resurfaces at times, in my opinion, even in *Shifting Involvements* (Cf., also, Adelman, 2013, ch. 14).

216 "Even though Rostow had coined what became the most popular metaphor (the 'take-off')," Hirschman wrote (1981a, p. 11), "he had really taken a monoeconomics position. For he [Rostow] divided the development process into his famous five 'stages' with identical content for all countries, no matter when they started out on the road to industrialization. Gerschenkron (1962, p. 355) derided the notion 'that the process of industrialization repeated itself from country to country, lumbering through [Rostow's] pentametric rhythm' and showed, to the contrary, how the industrialization of the late-coming European countries such as Germany and Russia differed in fundamental respects from the English industrial revolution, largely because of the intensity of the 'catching-up' effort on the part of the latecomers. Even though it was limited to nineteenth century Europe, Gerschenkron's work was of great importance for development economics by providing *historical* support for the case against monoeconomics" (emphasis Hirschman's).

217 This in fact helps make clear why Albert, in order to explain shifting involvements, took the path of consumption and not that of other important "shifts," such as those related to work, income, family, friendship, etc. Moreover, this episode retrospectively casts some doubt on the sincerity of the two arguments he offers the reader to clarify this choice: "First," he wrote (1982, p. 22), "a beginning had to be made somewhere; the task I had set myself was so novel and arduous that I could not aspire to breaking ground everywhere at once. Second, and more important, the occasional movement of large numbers of people into the public arena tends to have such momentous historical consequences that this particular shift [. . .] is of particular interest for the understanding of

Albert wonders,[218] "about the massive expansion in consumer durables that had indeed marked the postwar prosperity in the United States, and had rapidly spread to Western Europe, Japan, and elsewhere? Had he failed to see some dangerous portents in this expansion?" Clearly, these are rhetorical questions.

This also explains why, in order to get down to work, our author needed a jump-start on the theme of consumption (and consumerism)—which he found in Tibor Scitovsky's *The Joyless Economy* (1976), a book which, in its title alone, plainly turns the logic of Rostow's celebrations on its head. Indeed, a positive response to the questions just cited could be found, Albert continued,[219] in this "stimulating book that, without actually mentioning Rostow's positive account of the consumer durables boom, offered a new and highly original analysis of consumer satisfaction and dissatisfaction." To conclude, Hirschman accepted Scitovsky's gambit and committed himself to developing its reasoning, but in a new direction.[220]

(4) *The Joyless Economy*, as Hirschman recalled,[221] "was written in the aftermath of the student revolts and influenced me strongly. Right at the beginning of his book, Scitovsky refers starkly to its historical background: the downfall of American consumers from the brief (Rostowian) triumph they had celebrated at the middle of the twentieth century when they spent 'the world's highest income on the world's most copied and coveted life-style.' Within a decade, this self-image was to be largely destroyed, and Scitovsky asks: 'Could it be that we seek our satisfaction in the wrong things, or in the wrong way, and are then dissatisfied with the outcome?'[222] This question, of course, contradicted the traditional economic approach, according to which consumers know what is good for them and calculate expertly how to maximize their satisfactions. But Scitovsky protested against this simplistic and apologetic tradition and devoted

social change." As we can see, being silent about Rostow, and thus about why he favored that angle over others that were possible, was a choice that inevitably ended up making the argument less persuasive than it could have been.

218 Hirschman (1998, p. 12).

219 *Ibid*. Albert had probably met Tibor Scitovsky already in 1936, at the London School of Economics (Adelman, 2013, p. 122).

220 Scitovsky's interest was in fact centered on boredom, which he regarded as typical of wealthy societies, and on the "stimulations" that could alleviate it. Hirschman, on the other hand, takes up his reasoning from the standpoint of disappointment (Meldolesi, 1995, pp. 177–178).

221 Hirschman (1998, pp. 12–13).

222 Scitovsky (1976, pp. 2–4).

his first chapters to various complications and illuminating explorations in individual psychology. For me the most interesting distinction he developed was that between comfort and pleasure."

It is this distinction, in fact, that becomes in its turn a cornerstone of *Shifting Involvements*. "The human drives to relieve discomfort and to achieve comfort do make for pleasure in two ways. First of all, pleasure is generated by repeated travel from varieties of discomfort to *comfort* (e.g., from hunger to satiation). Second, pleasure occurs also as we move from inactivity or boredom to renewed activity, as a result of various types of *stimulation*. To the extent that countries become economically advanced and affluent, the first ingredient of pleasure—the journey from discomfort to comfort—is reduced or held at bay; hence stimulation should take over as a major source of pleasure. But with people being hardly conscious of the contrast between pleasure and comfort, they pursue the latter at the expense of stimulation and suffer a deficiency in overall pleasure." Even while intentionally leaving out many details and nuances, this brief description of Scitovsky's model, Albert argues, clearly shows "how it enabled me to produce my own story of successive disappointments," a paradoxical effect quite distinct from "the *expansion* of private consumption of durable goods."[223]

The main point, then, is that "in comparison with conventional purchases, new durable goods were more weighted with comfort than with pleasure. As a result, the first massive appearance of durables in a consumer culture will produce an 'initially disconcerting'[224] change in the traditional balance of pleasure and comfort." "As the new durables are increasingly taken for granted, the extra comfort and time they provide must be taken advantage of and be occupied by new forms of stimulation. In the absence of such stimulation, disappointment will set in. A large part of Scitovsky's book is devoted to these topics."[225]

Private and Public

(5) As Albert explained, his primary objection was Scitovsky's "utter neglect of the *public* dimension. He did not conceive of politics, participation in public

223 Hirschman (1998, p. 13; original emphasis). "An expansion," Albert points out, "that, just a short while ago, had been considered the essence of various 'economic miracles.'" As we can see, even retrospectively, in his memory, he intends to get to the bottom of Scitovsky's rebellion as it concerns Rostowian apologetics regarding consumer goods—and also, of course, consumption theory in economics.

224 Hirschman (1982, p. 34).

225 Hirschman (1998, p. 14).

life, pursuit of the public interest (or of 'public happiness,' in the language of the eighteenth century) as alternative sources of stimulation. I still believe it is worthwhile to explore such alternatives to a predominantly private life. But my original critique along these lines remained imprisoned in the two mutually exclusive categories of the private and the public. I failed to realize that there are important occasions when the public and the private meld and merge. In doing so I was perhaps merely following an ancient tradition. Take, for example, the biological function of filling one's stomach. This has long been considered a purely private activity that was contrasted with the pursuit of 'higher,' spiritual values and was often treated with disdain in comparison."[226]

The remainder of Hirschman's essay in point of fact concerns the meal—by way of an extraordinary intellectual jaunt through different eras, and an in-depth look at an important essay by Georg Simmel. But the informed (and hard-working) reader will not fail to notice, at this point, that *this example*, however significant and illuminating, does not by any means exhaustively cover the argument thus initiated. Indeed, we search impatiently (and in vain) for any clarifying cues that would permit the generalization of Hirschman's discussion, even gradually, to life's many "important occasions when the public and the private and meld and merge" (including those linked to the "fate" of the GDR recalled in ch. 1). Perhaps the reader will be inclined to conjecture about the possible directions in which such an issue might be developed, possibly concluding (pending confirmation) that by means of his deft "self-subversion" on commensality, Albert has made an entire field of thought available to scholars.

In any event, to actually verify whether or not this is the case requires calling to mind at this point a section of the trajectory of logic in *Shifting Involvements*. "The construction of any theory of cycles of collective behavior," Hirschman maintained, "must face a difficult task. To be persuasive [it] must be endogenous: that is, one phase must be shown to arise necessarily out of the preceding one [. . .], just as any useful business cycle theory must be able to show how the economic downturn or bust follows necessarily from the preceding upswing or boom and vice versa."[227]

226 *Ibid.*

227 Hirschman (1982 p. 4). "At most, my enterprise will have something in common with the Kondratieff cycle, whose duration is so long (50–60 years) that, given the limited historical experience with capitalism so far, we cannot be quite sure whether it really exists."

True enough. But how does this happen? "In spite of the large number of reviews," I wrote at the time,[228] "it seems to me that the spirit of *Shifting Involvements* was captured only in a statement from Daniel Bell (with the collaboration of Clifford Geertz) as president of the panel of judges for the Talcott Parsons Prize [. . .]." The book, he states, "takes as its starting point certain problems in the theory of consumer choice, characteristically turns these into an account of political participation, and ends by arguing that the two are actually a single social process, governed by hope and disappointment. What seems to be at first some small, if unconventional idea about 'changes in preference,' is shown to have unimagined facets and, in the fashion characteristic of Hirschman's work as a whole, it uncovers a larger idea that illuminates the way we live"—namely, that of shifting involvements.

I also argued that the essay by the late Guillermo O'Donnell (1986)[229] of thoughts on the Argentine experience that was written for the first Festschrift in Albert's honor (which he enjoyed) is an important addition to the book, not least because, as I wrote, "I have come to the conclusion that the Hirschmanian theory of the social cycle, once constructed, becomes *more* convincing when it is re-examined from within a concrete, dramatic and illuminating experience such as that of Argentina, and that perhaps we can go further down this road." My paper in fact showed how the argument could be developed further on the theoretical-practical level, taking as its starting point the intense period of social movements in the 1960s–1970s, in which Nicoletta Stame and I had participated.[230]

228 Meldolesi (1987a, p. 41); Bell (1983, p. 7). A similar judgment, but referring to Albert's entire opus, was recently expressed by Fernando Henrique Cardoso in a letter sent to the Hirschman Memorial (Vv.Aa., 2013, pp. 15–16). Cf. above, ch. 1, sec. 13.

229 "On the Fruitful Convergences of Hirschman's *Exit, Voice, and Loyalty* and *Shifting Involvements*: Reflections from the Recent Argentine Experience" (1986). We read, moreover, in a note Albert wrote for his daughter Lisa in 1998 (cf., below, ch. 4, n. 307): "My work experience with the Varian Fry Committee in Marseilles (June–December 1940) has helped me to understand some of the issues in Latin America—particularly those related to the violence which occurred later mostly in Brazil, Argentina, Uruguay, Chile." In part, this also most likely explains Albert's caution about certain characteristics of the youth movements of the 1960s.

230 Meldolesi (1987a, p. 39). I refer in particular to the fact that (*ibid.*, p. 46) the Hirschmanian theory of the social cycle, constructed, as noted above, as an endogenous, development-independent theory, once achieved, "can be introduced into an unbalanced"

(6) But apart from the undeniable interest in this approach and the achievement of some important results,[231] Albert's overall enterprise remained in doubt. *Shifting Involvements*, as I argued in 1994,[232] is a book "that aroused interest but cannot be said to have been properly understood. At the heart of the issue [. . .] is probably the "double-edged" nature of its conceptual framework. On the one hand, the thesis of disappointment and the social cycle allowed the Pandora's box of shifting involvements to be opened for the first time, but on the other hand, it is to some extent inadequate with respect to additional experience and the complexity of reality."

Although recent access to Hirschman's papers has not modified this view, it did allow me to peruse the very wide-ranging debate that preceded, accompanied and followed *Shifting Involvements*—undoubtedly one of our author's most closely observed and controversial books.

Many people, as Adelman noted,[233] found the book distant, speculative, too theoretical. This is understandable for a number of reasons. In the first place, the subject matter was still fresh in people's minds. Also, the book was addressed to a broad range of disciplines, and few could resist the temptation to "have their say," whether it had been thought through or not. In addition, Albert had intentionally raised the moral question arising from changing involvements (and called upon a generation—as becomes clear in the conclusions—to better calibrate their political commitment based on the answer). Furthermore, people had difficulty recognizing themselves in a theoretical analysis that was "imprisoned," as Hirschman eventually acknowledged, "in the two mutually exclusive categories of public and private."[234]

growth path—thus linking this text to other works by the author in order to analyze problems concerning development and democracy, participation opportunities, alternating delegitimization, successive stages of involvement, and political "tacking"—and to connect it to the powerful idea of the "principle of conservation and mutation of social energy" that Albert later proposed in *Getting Ahead Collectively* (1984a).

231 "The journey which I undertook," Albert wrote (1982, p. vii), "permitted a number of elaborate side trips which yielded, among many other observations, a critique of conventional consumption theory, a better understanding of collective action, and a new interpretation of the universal suffrage" (Meldolesi, 1994, pp. 307–308).

232 Meldolesi (1994, pp. 307–308).

233 Adelman (2013, pp. 552 and 564–566).

234 "Personally," as I myself wrote (1987a, p. 51), "I believe that the generation of the 1960s–70s was unable to embrace [*Shifting Involvements*] because they failed to truly identify with the author's conceptual novel."

Albert had accepted an invitation to host the Eliot Janeway Lectures in Historical Economics at Princeton University. "One of the purposes of these lectures, which I gave in December 1979 under the title *Private and Public Happiness: Pursuits and Disappointments*," he declares in the Preface, "is to honor the memory and intellectual heritage of Joseph Schumpeter. [. . .] Early, partial drafts of the essay were intensively discussed in seminars at the Institute for Advanced Study, at Stanford and Yale, and at the European University Institute in Florence. On and after these occasions, I have debated my points with a very large number of colleagues, orally as well as in correspondence."[235]

Perhaps embarrassed by the avalanche of comments he received, he decided to accept only a few of the suggestions[236] and to hedge somewhat by explicitly reducing the scope of the undertaking.[237] "What Hirschman did," Adelman wrote, "was to tack where he faced the least resistance. He elaborated the passages and arguments that were already strong. There were many more quotes from the classics. He added more detail on consumer theory as well as on theory and evidence of the history of political participation." He reinforced the bibliography. "He did address, albeit in a few paragraphs, the role of ideology in the making of meta-references and added a section based on his reading

235 Hirschman (1982, pp. vii–viii). Actually, the editor of the Princeton University Press had circulated the manuscript among various of the Press's consultants for comments. Cf. the report of these discussions (Adelman, 2013, ch. 18), which included (among many others) Robert Keohane, Quentin Skinner, Judith Tendler, Hirschman's daughter Lisa, Robert Lane, Joan Scott, George Akerlof, Claus Offe etc. At a certain point, Adelman observes (*ibid*., pp. 559 and 560), the "consensus" of friends and colleagues "seemed to call for a longer, empirically driven book. But this [*Shifting Involvements*] was not one of these. It was an 'essay,' or series of 'essays,' an analytical twist on the Montaigne tradition but pressing up against the limits of the genre." Nevertheless, as he goes on to state, "Hirschman's decision not to follow up on the quality and quantity of suggestions is hard to explain." Cf., however, n. 280 below.

236 Typically, his picture of the debate resulting from the preface to *Shifting* is more a response to the need to extricate himself. "Never before have I received so many excellent suggestions that just had to be incorporated." Hirschman wrote (1982, p. viii), "with the result that at times I felt I was turning from author into editor. [. . .] I am very grateful to all these excellent people for having thickened my plot." But without changing it, obviously. While at the beginning the passage in fact seems to suggest that the objections to the manuscript were accepted, it makes it clear as it goes on that many of them were not.

237 While this cannot have been an easy decision, in retrospect it does seem wise. For it was not until much later, with *Melding* (the essay we are discussing, on commensality), that Albert shows that he finally mastered the theme of shifting involvements—even if at that point he was unwilling (or perhaps unable) to rework it himself.

of Harry Frankfurt's distinction between first-order desires and second-order desires (that is, desires about desires). Cicero, too, per Skinner's suggestion, makes an appearance. But little of this was evidence of the kind his readers yearned for. It did not really address the more fundamental issue of how the oscillation between the two connected spheres was supposed to be explained, since this was the internal motion of his endogenous theory." "Hirschman dug in his heels and called the book 'a conceptual novel.'"[238]

To grasp this "change in atmosphere," it is sufficient to compare the openings of the two texts. "The only real restriction implicit in my mandate," Albert stated, in opening his lectures honoring the memory of Joseph Schumpeter,[239] "is that I be intellectually ambitious. So here is my alibi for the somewhat grandiose title that I have chosen for these lectures."[240] *Shifting Involvements*, on the other hand, begins as follows: "I am not sure that this book qualifies as a work of social science. It is so directly concerned with change and upheaval, both individual and social, that at times I had the feeling that I was writing the conceptual outline of a *Bildungsroman* (with, as always in novels, a number of autobiographical touches mixed in here and there)."[241]

Pending a careful study comparing the two texts point by point (and in the light of the numerous critical remarks now available in Albert's papers), one cannot help but note that between the two versions—the lectures and the published book—there is a gap, a change of gears, that is quite baffling[242] for several reasons.

238 Adelman (2013, pp. 562 and 563). "Page 114," Adelman adds (*ibid.*, pp. 562–563), "featured an image he found in the Bibliothèque Nationale of a worker giving up his gun and bullets to cast a ballot, with the suggestion that universal male suffrage was a way to channel the desires of an 'expressive' citizenry and thus give up the notoriously rebellious ways of Parisian rabble-rousers."

239 Hirschman (1979a, box 78, folder 1).

240 "Private and Public Happiness: Pursuits and Disappointments." The first part of the title is of eighteenth-century derivation and was subsequently used, not coincidentally, for the Italian edition—as if to say: my dear Italians, you of all people will be able to appreciate my message about happiness.

241 Although this was not enough, as it turned out, to head off the impression, supported in numerous critical reviews, that the analysis in *Shifting Involvements* had failed to convince its intended audience (cf. Adelman, 2013, pp. 563–564).

242 I remember that, in October 1986, I asked him about this "*diminutio*." Reversing the order of the addenda, he replied that he had needed to hurry because he had to give the lectures. It is an answer that "matches" the one he gave me when I later asked him what he thought of the protests of 1968. He replied that, having been absorbed that year in writing *Exit* (at Stanford's Institute of Behavioral Studies), he was unable to judge. That is

(7) In the first place, *Shifting* is not a book that fits in with a line of thought that was already mapped out, unlike several of his essays from the same time.[243] It undoubtedly represents one of Albert's "new forays" (to use the terminology from *A Propensity*),[244] not least because this was the first monograph Hirschman had published since writing (together with Geertz and other colleagues) the two programmatic papers referred to above in the Preface. And it is therefore likely that he intended, at least in moments of creative fervor, to assign it a function of "pathfinder" toward new horizons.

But the debate unleashed by the Schumpeter lectures was such that Hirschman decided to move, finally, onto another, more cautious track. Here it is important to bear in mind his well-known general avoidance of heated debates and his unwillingness to go out of his way to persuade his audience—it was simply not in his nature. Instead, he undertook to find ways out of the situations he found himself in. He may have been helped by the Colornian proposition that in addition to what it says, a text should be considered as a revealing reflection of the person who wrote it. And it may be that thinking back over the various stages that prompted the writing of *Shifting Involvements*, he hit upon the solution recalled above.[245]

In any case, if this is true, by confessing to the semi-autobiographical nature of the book, he also (more or less consciously) provided us with a valuable gateway to understanding another source of inspiration for the text (along with the desire to explain the major behavioral changes of the 1960s–1970s,[246]

to say that despite our friendship, there were occasions when Albert preferred an evasive answer to the truth—so strong was the desire in him to extricate himself, to *se debrouiller*, even at the cost of misleading someone. Not to mention his pretense of having a doctorate (PhD) from the University of Trieste (a claim Adelman repeats more than once in his biography), when in fact it was only a BA in economics. (Evidently, at some point, such a need to muddy the waters must have reached Sarah as well. She told me, in fact, that there were no more papers to study because Albert had been good not only at writing them, but at destroying them as well. Whereas now, 81 folders have emerged!).

243 I am thinking in particular of "A Generalized Linkage Approach to Development" (1977a) and "The Rise and Decline of Development Economics" (1981a).

244 Although reasoning based on oscillations was already present in his earlier work—for example, in the important Introduction to *A Bias for Hope* (1971) (cf. Meldolesi, 1987, 1995, ch. 3).

245 In any case, such an unusual "change of gears" speaks volumes about Albert's ability to keep himself always on the alert, with a receptive and typically modest attitude toward the signals coming to him from reality.

246 Hirschman (1982, p. 3).

the Rostow-Scitovsky question on consumerism, seeking "a better understanding of collective action," "a new interpretation of the universal suffrage"[247] etc.). A gateway, that is, that allows us, all things considered, to perceive a source of inspiration that Albert himself, at least initially, was not entirely aware of. This is that *at the time* he regarded his own life as marked by strong oscillation from public to private and back again—something which, incidentally, may now be seen, one phase after another, in Adelman's biography. Following Hirschman's marked prewar dedication to the public interest there was a contrary push toward the private side, which attracted him in his first American experience (and which he became even more aware of in the contrast when he swung back the other way, under arms). And then the private-public (pro-European) balance he achieved during the Marshall Plan period gave way to his private happiness in Colombia. Subsequently, his professional affirmation in the Ivy League yielded to a certain tendency toward re-politicization which, present in embryonic form as early as the 1950s, probably took hold gradually in the 1960s (with the Latin American coups and the emergence of social movements), and is notable in *Exit*.[248] And so on.

(8) In addition, the hypothesis could also be put forward that the emphatic polarization between private and public that Albert felt he had experienced in his life was probably responsible, at least in part, for his protracted inability to break free of the opposition between the two spheres—which afterward, at past the age of 80, he wished to abandon. This is the kind of reasoning that Eugenio Colorni would have considered anthropomorphic—in the sense that Hirschman, having himself perceived a need to focus alternately on the public or the private, attributed this . . . to "everybody."[249]

247 *Ibid*., p. vii. Cf. above.

248 Furthermore, at the end of Appendix B in Rodwin and Schön, eds. (1994, p. 321), we read that Hirschman, in conversation with the authors of this Festschrift, also made "another autobiographical declaration"—"he recounted how he had become an American 'patriot' as a result of World War II and his work on the Marshall Plan, and how in Latin America he began to be more critical, seeing the Alliance for Progress as 'too naïve and simple-minded.' These views were reinforced by 'the events of the 1960s,' when he saw other friends (Alexander Gershenkron in particular) turn conservative; he had often said he was 'grateful' to Latin America for having kept up or rekindling the 'ardors' of his youth."

249 Colorni (1998, part iv); and Colorni and Spinelli (2020, ch. 6). But the reasoning can also go the other way. That is to say, the polarization (within certain limits) of Albert's life, to the point of suggesting to him the thesis of changing involvements, can be considered a hidden blessing. In this way his "Bildungsroman" has managed to acquire a meaning that is both theoretically suggestive and educational for "everyone."

Perhaps this is exactly what happened. That is, Albert's original critique, as part of the balance sheet drawn up at that specific moment in his life, "was imprisoned in the two mutually exclusive categories of public and private." And he didn't realize *at the time* that "there are important occasions when the public and the private meld and merge"—something it is perfectly possible to see *after* the "Berlin exploit" discussed above, *after* his social, political, and human reconciliation with himself, and *after* he in a sense re-established the links between his first and his last politicization.

It's easy to see at this point, the importance to our argument of *Shifting Involvements* and the criticism finally offered in "Melding." Because engaging with late Hirschman, Germany, and today's Europe also allows us, *ipso facto*, to reason retrospectively not only about the tortuous path that characterized Albert's life and work, but also on the importance of his final self-subversions which, in expunging or correcting some lapsed aspects of his work, also manage (almost miraculously) to rebalance it as a whole—by means of the visual perspective he finally acquired.

The Logic of Commensality

(9) All this further explains why, in writing "Melding," Hirschman was able to limit his argument to the single example of the meal in order to explain the key idea that public and private mix and merge. As we saw in Chapter 1, he did know of other examples, and he would have had no trouble finding still others (large and small, exceptional and ordinary). But Albert needed to find something special—something in the public eye. Something so definitive as to become memorable—emblematic of our inability to see the processes of merging and melding between the two spheres and therefore maximally instructive for those who, like Hirschman himself, had long failed to see such possibilities.[250]

But perhaps there is also another reason. This essay got Albert out of the predicament that he had in a certain sense left suspended at the beginning of *Shifting Involvements*, as mentioned above. Because, even after the exceedingly eloquent explanation of the central point of the argument to be self-subverted, *Shifting* still remains useful in its own right. More than a theory in the strict sense of the term, it is a theorized possibility, arising from many needs and

250 And which, one might add, also lends itself to bringing down a (somewhat bittersweet) curtain on the "comedie humaine." See below, sec. 11 and n. 259.

concerns, and inspired by a life—that of its author. And furthermore, if one were to re-examine from this standpoint the heated debate surrounding Hirschman's lectures in honor of Schumpeter prior to the publication of *Shifting Involvements*, one would likely conclude that many of the remarks and objections put forward were rooted in the life experiences ... of those who proposed them.

For our purposes, then, it is best to resume the discussion from the more positive side of the text. I think, in fact, that the statement by Bell (and Geertz—two of Albert's friends) recalled above may be a good starting point for reconsidering the issue, focusing on the post-Berlin Wall papers that Hirschman left us.

In the first place, at the end of "Exit, Voice, and the Fate of the GDR," mentioned earlier,[251] Albert raises a methodological point that contains the most important self-subversive element in his argument and refers implicitly to *Shifting Involvements*. Thus, it is true that the extraordinary affair recounted in the essay in a sense represents a proven demonstration of the thesis that "in some momentous constellations, exit can cooperate with voice, voice can emerge from exit, and exit can reinforce voice,"[252] and that it therefore does not make sense to construct a rigid and immovable distinction between public and private.

And in less momentous constellations? And in general? These are questions that come from someone who in the meantime had got used to thinking "á la Hirschman"—that is in terms of differences, oppositions, and interrelations. In this regard, in my opinion, in the early 1990s, the intellectual outline of *Shifting* recalled by Bell was regaining strength in Albert's mind. I think, in fact, that the psychological (and emotional) "block" regarding social movements (youth movements especially) that can be glimpsed in the fabric of the 1982 book had by then been removed by his study of the dissolution of the GDR.

Consider, for example, the surprising (even in its title) "Social Conflicts as Pillars of Democratic Market Societies"—originally written as a background paper for the 100th session of the Bergedorf Discussion Circle held on November 13 and 14, 1993, in Dresden (in the recently liberated former East Germany).[253] Obviously, we are now far removed from Hirschman's somewhat

251 Cf., above, ch. 1, sec. 11.

252 Hirschman (1995, p. 43).

253 The Körber Foundation of Hamburg, organizers of the event, had suggested the title, "How much community spirit does liberal society require?" As will be obvious from my

mocking attitude toward "shifting involvements" (and the youth movements of the 1960s).[254]

(10) With these ideas in mind, I shall now return to the essay on commensality. In the introductory section, as we have seen, Albert carefully recalls the small idea, in Daniel Bell's words, at the beginning of *Shifting*. But then, instead of tackling a possible reworking of his reasoning of 15 years earlier, he entrenches himself in a remarkably evocative example that revisits some of the cornerstones of the history of human culture and civilization, and which (in my humble opinion) aims (although this is not explicitly stated) to inoculate Hirschman (and the reader) against the ever-recurring tendency to build a Chinese wall between public and private.

Let me summarize the core of the argument. "Both the Old and the New Testaments laid down the rule that 'man does not live by bread alone' [. . .]. It was far more important to follow the Lord's commands than to eat." Hence the praise for fasting in the late Middle Ages, which "became the essence of meritorious religious behavior" (especially for women), followed by the rediscovery of the pleasure of eating (and drinking) during the Renaissance, along with Montaigne's important stipulation that "one must look out not so much at what one eats as with whom one eats."[255]

But "the separation of the consumption of food from the so-called higher activities" was immediately reaffirmed by Pascal. In one of his *Pensées*, he contrasted believing in God with partaking in tangible goods—a distinction very close to the one between public and private goods used by contemporary economists. "Following Paul Samuelson's classic formulation in the 1950s," Albert explains, "private goods have been defined as those that are held and consumed individually, while public goods are those whose consumption and enjoyment by one citizen does not affect the quantity available to others [. . .]. Interestingly enough, the good that occurred to Samuelson to stand as a typical example of private goods was the loaf of bread [. . .], while the typical public goods were

introduction, Hirschman wrote (1995, p. 231, n.), "I start out with this question [. . .]. The bulk of the essay, however, deals with problems which, though related, are better epitomized by the title given here." Typically, while the essay starts with a question specific to the occasion (and German culture), it nonetheless opens up to a much broader social issue, the basis of our democratic market societies.

254 Cf., in this connection, my critical remarks on the conclusions of *Shifting*—Meldolesi (1987a, pp. 50–52).

255 Hirschman (1998, pp. 14 and 15).

such 'non-rival' services such as police protection, national defense, and public education."[256]

"When this distinction was first clearly made, in the immediate postwar period, public opinion about the role of the state was on the whole quite positive and public goods were celebrated, in spite of the intrinsic difficulties of estimating the demand for them." The economist thus "retained and reinforced the basic dichotomy of the Bible and of Pascal. Little attention was paid to goods that would somehow be intermediate between the private and the public category or would belong to both."[257]

(11) At this point, the argument suddenly changes course, and turns to Georg Simmel's "Die Soziologie der *Mahlzeit*"[258] [The sociology of the meal]—a brief but penetrating argument in which "a distinguished sociologist had called attention to situations where goods that seem to be wholly private actually have important collective dimensions." At almost the beginning of the essay, Hirschman is struck by a paragraph according to which communal mealtime represents "a bridge" between the private and public functions of eating and drinking. "Persons who do not share any interest can join in the common meal—in this possibility, mediated through the primitive and transparent character of material interest, *lies the immense sociological significance of the meal*[259]—in a word, 'commensality,' which etymologically refers to eating together around a table (*mensa*)."

"Simmel's basic insight about the meal providing a connection between two very different spheres—those of the selfish individual and of the social collective—leads him to throw light on various other ways in which eating has been 'civilized,' from the rules that were set for eating from the pot and later

256 *Ibid.*, pp. 15 and 16; and Samuelson (1954, 1955).

257 Hirschman (1998, p. 16 and 17). Note how this reasoning anticipates later interest in the commons, as found later in Elinor and Vincent Ostrom—Elinor's Nobel Prize included.

258 Simmel (1910). In German, *Mahlzeit*, as Albert explains (1998, p. 19), "has long been used also as an exclamation celebrating commensality at the beginning of the joint meal, as a term of benediction when a group sits down together to eat. The exclamation served as an abbreviation for the more religious invocation '*Gesegnete Mahlzeit!*' (May this meal be blessed)."

259 Simmel (1910; emphasis added by Albert). "I came across this article in German and was much taken by it several years ago. Thinking it had still not been translated [while actually it had been, as an appendix to Symons 1994], I decided to undertake this job in the spring of 1995 in Berlin. I am using my unpublished translation here."

from plates, to the use and manner of holding knife, fork and spoon, and even to the appropriate decoration of the dining room."[260]

Finally, "toward the end of his essay, Simmel characteristically moves in an unexpected direction. His story rises first from the natural-physical to the social-aesthetic. But in a final twist, Simmel interrupts or qualifies this ascent by noting that the basic need to eat does not permit a wholly free flow of conversation. Thus, he defends the 'banality of normal table talk' and sets a definite ceiling to the lofty and possibly controversial sphere to which the meal was almost about to take us."[261]

"Simmel's essay," Albert continues, bringing Simmel's reasoning into his own work,[262] "confirmed the positive light under which I had presented, in *Shifting Involvements*, the 'truly nondurable' goods—that is, those that, like food and fuel, are actually *used up* in the process of consumption. Influenced by Scitovsky's distinction between comfort and pleasure, I had thought that these goods would cause less disappointment than durables: food vanishes in the course of consumption and therefore permits the process of pleasure generation to start over again [. . .]. But it now seems likely to me," he adds, "that [. . .] I followed a correct instinct, but invoked inadequate reasons: I continued to look at eating and food intake as purely private and self-centered activities."

On the contrary, "the superiority of food over what I called 'possessions' is primarily rooted in Simmel's insight about the meal: it is the ease with which the private consumption of food is connected with collective or public

260 Hirschman (1998, p. 19). The prevailing image that emerges in this portrait of the meal is in my opinion that of the traditional bourgeois family ritual, in which distributive democracy is counterbalanced by the presence of the parents, who often, not surprisingly, use the occasion of commensality to get a sense of the situation. Here too, therefore, lies "the immense sociological significance of the meal." Norbert Elias, Albert continues, "wrote as an historical sociologist and was interested in the details of changing institutions and habit, whereas Simmel wrote as a social theorist and developed his ideas purely as deductions from general principles. Even the shape of the plate is thus deduced! Simmel derives its circular shape with a uniform radius from the principle that an identical portion of food is normally meant to be distributed to each participant in the meal and exclaims: 'The plates of a table do not tolerate any individuality.'"

261 *Ibid.*, pp. 19–20. Simmel, Albert later points out (p. 28), praises the banality of dinner table conversation (with its "generality and lack of intimacy") and advocates for its narrow boundaries—even against the hypocrisy and vulgarity characteristic of human and social relations that can arise at *Mahlzeit*. [The point is, I would add, that happily, one has the right to be a little evasive].

262 *Ibid.*, p. 20.

endeavors, due to commensality. Implicitly, Simmel compares eating with other basic physiological drives, such as sleeping, and he finds that among them only the intake of food is performed in common and therefore will lead to 'essential communal actions': it is the 'frequent experience of being together' and the 'habit of joining in a common purpose' which make for the 'immense sociological importance of the meal.'" It appears, Hirschman concludes,[263] "that in disregarding the Simmelian shift from the private to the public domain through the common meal, we have failed to recognize the substantial *external benefits* of this type of food consumption."

Beyond *Shifting*

(12) This is fine as far as it goes, the informed reader (familiar with *Shifting Involvements*) might object, but what are the actual consequences of this reasoning for the book's theoretical approach? If it is true, as we have just read, that there is a shift from the private to the public sphere in the very unfolding of the communal meal, shouldn't the theoretical analysis of "shifting involvements" be reopened *with this in mind*? Indeed, when it is recognized that sometimes respective preferences for the private and public spheres can mix and merge, it is clear that the pattern of the oscillations between the two spheres relates only to the *predominance* of one over the other, that these oscillations generally take on an irregular pattern, and that this pattern can no longer be interpreted in terms of a social cycle in the strict sense. So we have to work from a double script—on the one hand, the ever-present tendency to oscillation, and on the other hand, the continuous and often erratic deviations from that tendency.

This was not the road taken by Hirschman. Instead, he devoted the rest of the essay to two particularly interesting historical explorations, "Banqueting and Democracy" and "Symposium, *Männenbund*, and Beer Drinking in German Student Corporations." The arresting thesis of the former is that in ancient Greece, "apparently, equal division of the ritually sacrificed oxen among banquet members led in Athens, through a remarkable association of ideas, to the equal distribution of offices among the citizens through lottery."

Therefore, Albert concludes, "it would seem that Simmel was right: if Athenian democracy was one of its externalities or side-effects, the sociological-political significance of the meal or banquet was truly immense."[264]

263 *Ibid.*, pp. 20–21.
264 *Ibid.*, pp. 24 and 25.

In this way "a bloody religious sacrifice had a remarkable and remarkably positive outcome in the field of politics. But this relationship cannot he expected to have been the rule."[265] And so, characteristically, to make this point clear (before an Austrian audience) he presents a contrasting example that takes its lead from "Symposion and *Männerbund*"—an essay by Oxford Hellenist Oswyn Murray[266] emphasizing the structural similarities between the two institutions, Greek and Germanic. "Strangely," Hirschman observes, "Murray does not mention the spectacular contrast between the socio-political connotations and characteristics of symposium and *Männerbund*: the dawn of democracy in classical Greece, on the one hand, and the raging [. . .] fury of wild, plundering bands of young men [. . .] in ancient Germany and Scandinavia, on the other. One cannot help thinking of the *Männerbund* as foreboding some of the worst aspects of Germany's later political developments, such as the murderous activities of the post-1918 'Free Corps' and the subsequent SA and SS movements of the Nazi period."[267]

The conclusion is that "while they are consuming food and drink, people gathering for the *Mahlzeit* engage in conversation and discussion, exchange information and points of view, tell stories, perform religious services, and so on. From a purely biological point of view, there is no doubt that eating has a straightforward relationship to individual welfare.[268] But once they are done *in common*, eating and drinking normally go hand in hand with a remarkably diverse set of public or collective activities. That is why 'taking commensality seriously'—as Pauline Schmitt Pantel has urged[269]—is easier said than

265 "In a book on development projects" (Hirschman, 1967, ch. 5), Hirschman recalled, "I have made much of the 'centrality of side-effects.' The story I have just told about Greek banquets illustrates this concept." But, unfortunately, the result may also turn out to be negative.

266 Murray (1982).

267 Hirschman (1998, p. 26).

268 For an economist, the relief of hunger and the pleasure of eating are "a positive but decreasing function of spending on food. In the middle of the nineteenth century, the German statistician Ernst Engel (1821–96) demonstrated this functional relationship, and it seemed so reliable that it soon became known and celebrated as 'Engel's Law.' But to confine the consequences of food intake solely to the concurrent biological process of satiation," Albert comments (*ibid.*, p. 28), "means overlooking the considerable public dimension of commensality."

269 "The venerable existence and importance of the Greek banquet with its religious sacrifices has long been known [. . .]. A comprehensive treatise was published recently by the Hellenist Pauline Schmitt Pantel, under the title *La Cité au banquet: Histoire des repas*

done. The social, political, and cultural consequences of the common meal are extraordinarily varied; moreover, their outcome can turn out to be positive or negative. The common meal or banquet contributed to the 'invention' of democracy in the age of classical Athens, on the one hand; in the Imperial Germany of Heinrich Mann,[270] on the other, commensality could lead to the degradation of human relations and political life."

(13) This, then, is Albert's finish line. And, of course, we have no way of knowing what he would have written had he been able to continue his work.[271]

It is clear, however, that in late Hirschman, the now-achieved self-subversion—as in the conclusions of "Exit, Voice, and the Fate of the German Democratic Republic," and "Melding the Public and the Private Spheres: Taking Commensality Seriously"—had brought about a change in his *overall* perspective, from which "shifting involvements" could be observed as well.

It is therefore worthwhile to look at the topic again, to "elucubrate" over it, hypothetically, in an effort to better understand what Albert might reasonably have meant in his analyses (and, conversely, what we might suggest if we could still talk to him).

First of all, "Melding the Public and the Private Spheres" is an admirable essay, finished as Hirschman was just coming to terms with the exhaustion of his extraordinary intellectual abilities. As we have seen, his central point—that a clear separation of the private and public spheres must be dropped—represents the self-subversion of a key aspect of *Shifting*.[272] Otherwise, however, he clearly confirms the existence of "shifting involvements" and the validity

publics dans les cités grecques (1992) [. . .]. This rich work presents the evolution, over a period of almost ten centuries, of the banquet among the Greeks" (Hirschman, 1998, p. 29).

270 The reference here is, in fact, a well-known short story by Heinrich Mann, "Der Untertan" (The Subject), in which "the social psychology of communal drinking (rather than eating) is penetratingly explored. This story takes place in Imperial Germany just before World War I" (*ibid.*)

271 I am quite certain that he was no longer *able* to continue due to a fall in the mountains in the summer of 1995 (see, above, n. 16 in the Preface) at the age of 80. Albert hit his head, causing a cerebral hematoma; this led to increasing difficulty in continuing his work; and a few years later to severe physical decline. Nicoletta Stame and I stayed in touch with his wife Sarah and sister Eva and we visited Albert regularly for a long time—an "annual visit"—Sarah called it a bit ironically. We would rent a car in Boston and drive up the east coast to Princeton—for as long as he recognized us.

272 Which his thesis of the social cycle is based on in the book. Cf., above, sec. 5 and n. 227.

of the Scitovskian economic theory of consumption based on the difference between pleasure and comfort (and thus potential dissatisfaction) which he developed and extended to the public sphere.

What does all this mean?

It is true, first of all, that the essay contains a retrospective recognition that some of the criticism he received at the time (and aristocratically rejected) did, if nothing else, have some underlying justification which in the end emerged. In addition, in Albert's late democratic turnaround in favor of social movements (and commensality), what he *does not* say is important as well, alongside what he does. Here, if I am not mistaken, lies the somewhat secret, implicit aspect of the self-subversion of *Shifting Involvements*.

Why, one wonders, did Hirschman not embark on a reworking of his theory? Was it because he was no longer able to (one might conjecture) or, more reasonably, was it perhaps because he didn't think it necessary (and it wouldn't have been his style in any case)?[273]

Of course, as in the case of *The Strategy* and *Exit* (as well as *National Power* and *The Rhetoric*[274]), the self-subversion of *Shifting*, once exposed, requires a certain logical reordering of the fabric of the text. But, in this case, it is a key relationship that is "subverted"—that between public and private, which is precisely what shifting involvement depends on. And here it seems to me that without saying so explicitly, Albert meant to suggest to the readers of *Shifting* (who so desired) to pursue the argument themselves, at their leisure. It is as if he had written, "My contribution stops here. I've had my say—now you have yours."

(14) Let's take an example. We can pick the discussion up again with a passage from Simmel such as the following: "What I think, I can let others know about; what I see, I can show to others; what I say can be heard by hundreds of others—but what is eaten by a single person can under no circumstances be eaten by anyone else."[275] Despite this, as we have seen, eating—a private activity par excellence that concerns the isolated individual—instead has vastly important social consequences when it is practiced in common. If even a personal activity like eating can have such significant social implications, might not this be the case for others as well? Doesn't it then suggest that durable goods, which—as *Shifting* argues—easily become a source of (durable) disappointment, can also

273 Cf., above, ch. 2, n. 177.

274 A text known to have been subverted in the making by its own ch. 6.

275 Simmel (1910, cit. in Hirschman, 1998, p. 18).

be "status symbols"? Isn't it the case that in American culture, the middle-class display of material wealth (house, car, other durables) used to symbolize success (and in large measure, at first glance at least—still does)?

Sic stantibus rebus, it then becomes likely that the "disappointment with durable goods," which turns out to play such an important role in Hirschman's conception, not only concerns the material aspect of the merchandise (which may work just fine) or the shift from pleasure to comfort that follows its purchase, but also can represent (even unconsciously) the fact that as time goes on, one's own, legitimate private-public aspirations become frustrated, the collective recognition one counted on has waned, or the rate of personal and social freedom and emancipation has declined, and so on—so much so that one's domestic "setup," however comfortable, does not yield the expected satisfaction.

In other words, Hirschman constructed a conception of the social cycle of shifting involvements on the exclusively economic grounds (however unusual) of a new Scitovskian- Hischmanian theory of consumption. Later, however, he realized that communal eating has enormous social significance. Logically, this should have led him to reformulate the theory of shifting involvements on both economic and social grounds at once—thus reconnecting his reasoning with the extensive social literature on the subject, mainly American, from the 1950s and 1960s.

I am not in a position to assure the reader that this conclusion, which to me appears implicit in Albert's reasoning, was intentionally intimated or not. Possibly, he thought it was too obvious to be stated explicitly—better to leave it to the intelligence of the reader ("a word to the wise . . ."). Or perhaps he was just not in a hurry to haul in the net he had constructed.[276] But it is more likely that if I had suggested this exit route to him, he would have replied that it is just one of the possible evolutionary paths that the intricate history of life keeps up its sleeve. And undoubtedly, from this point of view, the importance of "Melding" with respect to a text like *Shifting*, cogent in its own way, is indeed that it opened a Pandora's box of a hundred possibilities.[277]

276 There is a suggestion of this, for example, toward the end of "Melding" where he distinguishes between useful and harmful inconveniences.

277 Consider, for example, the economic consequences of "fashions," the American obsession with the "brand new," or, conversely, the British tendency to repaint in perpetuity what one owns (trends that basically represent socioeconomic consumption alternatives that are within the reach of every consumer). Or think of the ebbs and flows and the

In fact, I still believe what I wrote at the time. Namely, that Hirschman's paper "has such a pioneering character that it effectively invites a multiplicity of analyses differing in perspective and in the historical experience they refer to." Moreover, as I wrote, "it is possible to identify disappointment across experiences in different sectors—in the consumption of durable goods, at work or in family attachments—while it remains largely impossible to derive *from any one of them* a change in general behavior."[278]

Indeed, at this point I would add that on the evidence of the many contributions to the discussions surrounding *Shifting*, both before and after its publication, it was clear even at the time that (generally) changes in behavior respond to a multiplicity of causes.[279] Thus, viewed from different angles, the construction of the social cycle contained in *Shifting*, however striking and historically challenging it may have been, appears nevertheless to be an expression of *one* of many possibilities (and a rather extreme one at that).[280]

But Albert stuck with his story. As mentioned, even many years later he saw his analysis concerning the disappointment of durable consumer goods as valid.[281] Probably not so much to preclude the existence of other processes, as because it was the one that felt valid—instructive for the reader and rooted in his own life. "I had my hands full," said to Offe in 1988, "making one 'endogenous' transition plausible; and I merely want to show the possibility of a phenomenological portrayal of that transition without affirming that the ones I am portraying are the only ones."[282]

myriad deceptions of political life ... And then, of course, beyond consumption, the shifting involvements concerning age, gender, production (work, profession), family life, leisure, etc.

278 Meldolesi (1987a, pp. 53 and 43; emphasis added). "In fact," I pointed out, "the researcher who insists on this path—in the conviction that change stems from the disappointment of consumption, from relations of production, or between the sexes—is up against ... a mirage."

279 But this is also true of the attraction of public life (with the hope of being able to influence it), disappointment in the emptiness of consumption, and the active pursuit of human satisfaction and happiness. It is also true that the realm of private consumption and the public arena are uneven, that the individual cycle is one thing, the collective cycle another, etc. (cf. Adelman, 2013, pp. 555–560).

280 And this explains, in retrospect, why Hirschman wanted at the time to view it, finally, as a conceptual novel. It is therefore not as "hard to explain" as Adelman maintains (*ibid.*, p. 560). Cf., above, n. 235.

281 Cf., above, sec. 2 and ff.

282 Hirschman (1988; box 75, folder 4).

So that if we go back to Bell's observation[283] on *Shifting* (according to which a small idea "about 'changes in preference,' is shown to have unimagined facets and, in the fashion characteristic of Hirschman's work as a whole, it uncovers a larger idea that illuminates the way we live"), we realize that this happens not through successive generalizations, but through a variety of other cognitive means—such as suggestion, mirroring, differentiation, inspiration.

And, therefore, this is why, in the Preface to *Shifting*,[284] after noting that he had never received so much good advice, Hirschman was able to write, "Perhaps this wealth of good advice stems from the character of the book, from its coming close to being a 'conceptual novel.' Everyone who read the early fragments wanted the hero to behave a bit differently or had a different explanation for his or her actions."

To Sum Up

(15) I agree with Adelman on one key point—*Shifting Involvements* is a "brave book." Albert's intention was "representing actors as neither heroes nor victims, but rather as fallible choosers muddling through imperfect alternatives. The politics of his argument was made explicit at a conference at Berkeley in March 1980, just as he was revising his manuscript. He asked himself, 'What was so *moral* about my inquiry?' When he got to the podium, he explained how Princeton students were rather 'shocked' by the original happiness lectures. Students were more accustomed to learning about human nature in terms of 'the rational actor beloved by economists.' When Hirschman presented Man as 'a blundering idealist, someone with interests *and* passions,' it sounded to them as a moral observation. Either-or commonplaces made Hirschman's kind of stories appear muddled and confused. Really, what Hirschman wanted was a human actor 'as a more lovable character, somewhat pitiable, but also a bit frightening—hence tragic.' "[285]

283 Cf., above, sec. 5 and n. 228.

284 Hirschman (1982, p. viii).

285 Adelman (2013, pp. 564–565). At the end of the cover-blurb of the Italian edition of *Shifting* (which Albert certainly approved and perhaps suggested) we read: "While in economic theory the analysis of the behavior of the 'rational subject' is dominant by far, in this book the author is concerned with humans who make mistakes, who reconsider, who adjust their preferences and desires to changing needs. In this way, Hirschman offers space for human complexity, reestablishing contact between common sense and

This is the point. Because "this tragic character sometimes needed some help." This, in fact, is the responsibility of the intellectual who must be constructive, the guardian of voice, even when it is atrophied. Who must "help the fallible citizen, this imperfect subject, to imagine alternatives without making them impossible." This, as Adelman comments,[286] "was a big idea that would consume him for years to come."

Here, then, we sense Hirschman's growing concern about the path the United States was then taking—and we get a sense, in the end, of what he would begin to devise shortly thereafter, just before taking the path that would lead him to *The Rhetoric* (1991).[287]

As for myself, I got involved with *Shifting Involvements* just as I had with Albert's experiences—from before and after the war.[288] In both cases, my research sought to ascertain the way things had actually been. While this was conditioned, obviously, by the absence of key information, this nevertheless did not keep me from sensing Hirschman's direction of travel, as just noted.[289]

Accordingly, I set about comparing my own experience with what I felt I had understood, and in the mid-1980s I found a working *modus vivendi* with Albert, a way for me to work alongside him, tracking (as far as I was permitted) the evolution of his work, writing a series of essays on the subject,[290] preparing the publication of some of his books in Italian,[291] and gradually constructing

economic analysis—which, due to the latter's long process of refinement, has perhaps faded." [Is this an editorial understatement?]

286 Adelman (2013, p. 565).

287 On December 1, 1991, Robert Heilbroner wrote to Albert regarding *The Rhetoric*, "Courage. I have not read anything so outspoken—imagine, naming names!—for years. I admired the book enormously." And Hirschman replied (December 17), "It looks more and more like you are quite right: the book seems to get some (pretty powerful) people terribly upset." (Box 75, folder 3).

288 Cf. sec. 2, and ch. 2, n. 101.

289 Which was further enriched by *Getting Ahead Collectively* (1984). (On a possible relationship between this text and *Shifting*; see Meldolesi, 1987a, pp. 50–52).

290 If I think back to numerous essays from that period (Meldolesi, 1985, 1985a, 1987, 1987a, 1987b, 1990a, 1991–1992, 1992a, 1994a), it is clear to me that they disencumbered a path between my study notes on Hirschman's work and bringing my own eventual contribution into focus.

291 Hirschman (1987, 1988a, 1990a, 1990b). From this perspective my role was similar to that of Claus Offe's for Germany. But taking into account the disparity in location, my role was in reality different. Because, from the vantage point of my "posting" in Naples, the need to learn in order to put things into practice inevitably took precedence. And this

Alla scoperta del possibile. Il mondo sorprendente di Albert O. Hirschman [Discovering the possible. The Surprising World of Albert O. Hirschman]—and in this way preparing a new launch of these ideas in the Italian South.[292]

This is the period when Albert was, on balance, pleased that I was concentrating on him. When he introduced me to third parties, he said (with a chuckle) that I was interested in a most interesting subject: him! This did not mean, however, that my true practical intentions intrigued him—the intellectual responsibility that he had decided to take on did not go so far as to alter his Princetonian habits. Instead, it was clear that in terms of geographical location, professional status, teaching, and individual inclination, I would be acting fundamentally on different ground. Indeed, I was looking for useful connections in Hirschman's work so that I could set up new projects at home.

prevented me from really taking part in the discussions on the frontiers of knowledge that Albert himself was promoting and in which, depending on what he was working on, he, from time to time, invited scholars from different countries to participate. Fortunately, at the time, protected by the "hiding hand" (Hirschman, 1967, ch. 1), I was not fully aware of this reverse side of the coin.

292 I am alluding, obviously, to the admittedly vague interest at the time in Hirschman's work on the part of the Cassa per il Mezzogiorno (and the somewhat unfortunate translation of *The Strategy*). By the time I met him, Albert had already made contacts with a view to re-opening a path for himself in Italy. He had published (not very successful) translations of *The Passions* (Feltrinelli), *Exit* (Bompiani) and *Shifting* (il Mulino). (The latter at my suggestion, was later revised, and the book was republished.) Moreover, as editors of his works, Hirschman had turned to Andrea Ginzburg (first) and Marcello de Cecco (later). For different reasons, both of them facilitated my meeting Albert, and I am grateful to them.

· 4 ·

A NEW APPROACH IN THE MAKING*

(1) Albert Hirschman's ideas, Fernando Henrique Cardoso wrote[293] "are instruments which, if utilized with art, modesty, and passion, help us to recognize new facts, to interpret them and to illuminate portions of history and even to construct sequences. Without turning them at the same time into a straight-jacket which would resist the facts." I believe that learning and developing the peculiar turn of mind that Albert employed is of great significance. Something that should be disseminated everywhere: *urbi et orbi.*

Albert was a policy-oriented man. While putting together a collection of papers for publication,[294] I was struck by something that he said to me some time ago[295]—"any idea that is not encouraging is faulty." Was it the voice of

293 * Under the title "Learning to Learn: some observations" (and in an abridged version), the first section of this chapter was written (originally in English) at the request of Joan Scott as a contribution to Vv.Aa, *A Bias for Hope* (2013).
Cardoso (1996).

294 Under the title *Imparare ad imparare* [Learning to Learn] (2013), a book dedicated to the memory of Albert Hirschman. (The quotation referred to above was used as its epigraph.)

295 It was probably around the turn of the century, when I was working for the Presidency of the Council of Ministers as chairman of the Committee on the Emergence of Non-regular Employment, or shortly before—when my leaning toward a full commitment in favor of regular employment had already become apparent. I remember that we were walking

his alleged optimism? I doubt it. I think he meant that regardless of your predictions for the future (positive or negative), the point is that you should know what to do, even in dreadful conditions (as Albert's story reminds us).

Therefore, from a human perspective, we should *not* be discouraged. We should not despair. We simply cannot afford it. Good ideas are those that encourage you to act in a correct way. They are part of Albert's "possibilism," that is, of his effort to enlarge the spectrum of human choices so that we can effectively improve our performance.

Of course, Albert had learned from Eugenio Colorni that, in scientific work, we should keep our feelings in check (our "anthropomorphism"). But he also learned that the human touch cannot be wholly eliminated from what we are doing—contrary for instance to the assumptions of so much of economics as generally taught all over the world. The bare "object of the exercise" of even the most abstract analytical notion (i.e., the reason for making the effort to invent it or learn it) should be recognized for what it is—an attempt to improve (openly or surreptitiously) the world we are actually in.[296]

Therefore, analysis and policy, Albert believed, go hand in hand.

Learning from Albert over a long period of time is an experience that I shared initially with a "happy few" (Fernando Henrique included) and one that I tested and circulated among students and friends for many years. To the Hirschmanian propensity "against parsimony"[297] it may be added that, in my experience, the *more ways* of doing things one finds and tries out in learning from Albert, the better.

After all, in the daily debates of 1937–1938 with his mentor (Eugenio Colorni), the young Hirschman was applying what he was learning to different fields (even going so far, in that initial *Sturm und Drang*, as to invent a theorem of statistics that . . . had already been invented!)[298]

One might aim to learn the way he learned—gradually acquiring both a degree of modesty, ingenuity and skill in processing facts, and substantial inventiveness in developing them and, of course, pondering them.

together outdoors, perhaps at the Institute for Advanced Study. Albert took my arm and (typically) in a low voice said these precise words, which I have memorized, exactly. Perhaps his specific intention was to encourage the activity I was about to undertake with my co-workers. But the statement struck me *precisely because of its general meaning.*

296 Cf., on this subject, Colorni (1998); Colorni and Spinelli (2020, ch. 6).

297 I refer here to Albert's well-known article (1984b).

298 Cf. Meldoledi (2013, ch. 1).

On the other hand, one might instead follow an "inverted sequence"[299]—even in learning—asking oneself Jean-Claude Casanova's question: "What would Albert think of this new problem that I face?"[300] Or one might follow the many linkages that connect, and sometimes subvert, his work (and/or ours). No matter the road taken, however, it must be kept in mind that generally speaking, outcomes in the process of learning are not "once and for all"—often they are a prelude to new developments, sometimes suggested by historical evolution. Take for instance the "infinitely naive proposals"[301] which allowed the older Albert to free himself from some of the political propositions suggested by his younger self. Of course, some of the groundwork for this can be found in his 1978 paper "Beyond Asymmetry."[302] But after Albert's spirited engagement in Berlin following the fall of the Wall, one may ask: would it have been conceivable without that previous "infinite naiveté"?[303]

My answer would be no, it wouldn't have.

An Omnipresent Question

(2) "I have always worked for Europe."[304] This was a recurring declaration of Hirschman's, so explicit and so often repeated as to (paradoxically) require clarification. After all, it is obvious that a major intellectual as cautious and measured as Albert would not want to leave any doubt on the subject. What he meant by such kind of expressions was that during his long, industrious and creative life, he had always contributed in one way or another—in his

299 A reference, obviously, to ch. 5 of *The Strategy* (1958)

300 See the *laudatio* of Jean-Claude Casanova (1990) at Albert's honorary degree ceremony at Sciences Po in Paris.

301 Hirschman (1978; now in 1981, p. 28).

302 My assessment of this is in Meldolesi (2013, ch. 2).

303 Both Colorni (1998) and Hirschman (1963) consider naiveté (or innocence) the starting point for learning.

304 "I have never stopped working for Europe," he declared, for example to the *Corriere della Sera* (January 5, 1987), "just like my brother-in-law Altiero Spinelli. Ever since I was a young Marshall Plan official trying to convince the Americans that the Common Market was not a danger to the peace" (cf., above, ch. 2, secs. 2–5). The implicit reference is to Hirschman's lecture at the State Department "Approaches to Multilateralism and European Integration" (1950)—the visionary text that later, in all probability, Albert wanted to shield more than any other from indiscreet American eyes. (cf. ch. 2, ns.) Conclusion: among Hirschman's many stratagems, he was using differences between national milieus, languages and cultures for his own purposes.

own way—to the construction of Europe, which meant progressively moving beyond the nationalism and war (and intransigence) that had been the causes of so much trouble.

On the other hand, in my opinion, to bring Hirschman's experience into focus, we need to frame it as part of a broader journey, one that includes the entire process of the gradual shaping of European unification. As a very brief example of what I have in mind, it is worth linking this experience to some objective data. To understand the issue of European unity as a cultural and political need, in fact, we have to go back at least to the nineteenth century (to Cattaneo, Mazzini, and Garibaldi). As a much-needed response to German expansionism (which was definitively upsetting the traditional balance—and balancing act—among the various European powers), we can trace it at least to World War I (explains Jean Monnet, who just at that time, *in corpore vili*, launched his key thesis of "uniting the peoples of Europe, not the states"[305]). As an avantgarde political activity, the battle for European unity actually began to show itself between the wars, mainly by way of anti-fascism. For the first actual steps toward unity, we must look to the era that accompanied and followed the Marshall Plan. And as a European Community, we must turn to the now historical process we are familiar with, which finally led to the European Union, to us.

In other words, taking a *long* look at a tortuous process as it labors to get underway, in successive stages, is important in clarifying the actual object of our discussion, including (of course) Hirschman's assertion quoted above.

In this light, I can confirm that throughout his adult life, for around 70 years, Albert never failed to contribute, from progressively differing vantage points, to the central, medium and long-term problem of the pursuit of European unity. This intriguing point of view *sic et simpliciter* gives credit to Hirschman as an actor (and privileged witness) in certain significant phases of this impressive trajectory—with all its still unresolved problems and a long way, as we know, from full and truly convincing solutions.

(3) First, we need only recall that "asked in a questionnaire of which achievement in his life he was most proud, Hirschman listed his work with the Italian anti-Fascists and with Varian Fry first, before his academic work on development in Latin America, and his books and articles."[306] This political starting point can be placed at the heart of Albert's ubiquitous commitment to Europe.

305 Monnet (1976, ch. 3).
306 Coser (1984, p. 163).

Furthermore, we saw at the beginning of Chapter 2 the intelligent determination of the Hirschman of the Marshall Plan in supporting the pro-European wing of the American delegation and contributing significantly to the development of its ideas.[307] Finally, at the end of that experience, he agreed to work for the government of Colombia and there discovered his intellectual way forward, which led him to the great American universities (and the Institute for Advanced Study); and to writing numerous, successful monographs and collections of essays. These in turn, in both genesis and objectives (direct and indirect), were inevitably affected by his training and interests.

When we return, therefore, with all this in mind, to the two brief programmatic texts from 1977 (mentioned in the Preface) that Albert composed at Princeton with Geertz and other colleagues, it is no surprise that for inspiration these turn favorably to European culture. To approve analysis of social phenomena as generally practiced in America, "with the usual categories of statistical and nomological explanation," *Our View of Social Science* argues, "is to give an unwarranted priority to the externalities of behavior, its etiology and regularities. This is not to deny, of course, that these approaches are essential, [. . .] but [. . .] a full understanding of most social phenomena requires that [. . .] at least as much attention should be paid to the linguistic, conventional, ritual and other symbolic systems in terms of which the agents and groups we study in the human sciences in fact describe, theorize about and appraise their own conduct. [. . .] In our opinion, no satisfactory account of social change is possible without careful consideration of changes in the frameworks of meanings that inform social action. This emphasis, we feel, recognizes some of the most interesting recent developments in the human sciences. Strong challenges to the modes of explanation characteristic of much of American social science

307 It should be added, on the other hand, that after his fall in the mountains in 1995 (cf., above, n. 16 of the preface and n. 271 of ch. 3), his daughter Lisa, a psychologist, convinced her father, as an exercise, to answer some of her questions in writing. Thus, on September 24, 1998 (box 3, folder 1) Albert wrote: "I spent a large part of the post-war period working on the European Payment Union. I continued to be absorbed by this interest and in 1949–50 was very active looking at how Altiero's permanent interest in European unification could be brought together with the American position that could be coordinated with those of Ambassador Bruce in Paris and of his collaborator William Tomlinson in Paris (the Paris financial attaché) with whom I had established a close relationship during the last phase of EPU relations and of French economic policy. This new phase of Bruce activism occurred when Bruce moved to Brussels to be in charge of the common policy of coal and steel." But then his friend, William Tomlinson, died.

have recently been issued by German phenomenology, French structuralism and several allied intellectual movements of increasing importance."[308]

And it is true that, in an efforts to rein in the predominance of ultra-liberal American culture, which was to become compelling in later years, Albert would increasingly draw on a European cultural inspiration that turned toward the humanities (rather than the natural sciences) and that probably had been behind his own move from Harvard to Princeton.

(4) All this strikes me as enlightening in terms of understanding the developmental process of the author's thinking.

First of all, as Geertz and Hirschman explain in *Our View of Social Science*, this is because the Institute, thanks to the presence of scholars from different disciplines and because it welcomes young American and foreign researchers,[309] was in a strategic position to perform this role of absorbing and developing new ideas.[310]

308 School of Social Science (1977, pp. 8–9). "A no less strong challenge," the passage continues, "to the belief in the possibility of a value-neutral social science has arisen out of the recent revival of Marxist social philosophy, as well as from the work of Kuhn and his followers. As a consequence of these inquiries into the logical and epistemological foundations of social science, there is now a growing interest in a purely hermeneutic view of the social disciplines (such as espoused by Ricoeur, Gadamer, Charles Taylor and many others) and in a frankly normative social theory (as in the work of Habermas and others of the Frankfurt School)."

309 "The type of social science to which we are committed," this text continues (*ibid.*, pp. 10–11), "seems to us admirably fitted to the predominant intellectual aspirations and traditions of the Institute as a whole. It also enables us to maximize the special opportunities available here. Our view of social science is at the moment more widely accepted in Europe than in America—especially in France, Germany, Italy and to some extent in England. It is thus crucial to furthering our aims that we should be able, as we currently do, to bring groups of scholars from all these countries (and from elsewhere, of course) to mix with the social scientists who come here from universities in this country." (Nicoletta Stame and I were able to be a part of this process thanks to the hospitality of Marcello de Cecco, who had been admitted to the Institute as an annual visitor. Beginning during that stay, Marcello, together with Francesco Asso, edited *Potenza nazionale* [National Power] 1987, a collection of texts on international, European and Italian economics that Albert had written at the height of World War II).

310 "There are many signs," adds this text, "that these new approaches are beginning to have some impact on American social science: the influence of Kuhn and the post-empiricists can be clearly discerned in much of the best recent history and sociology of science; the methods of hermeneutics have been adopted and developed by a new school of symbolic anthropology; the traditional models of rational economic man, and the framework of

Moreover, even as he assumed this function, Albert's cultural influence had been growing considerably in the developed world during the 1970s and 1980s. He was no longer just an expert in development and Latin America. Texts such as *Exit* and *The Passions,* transcending the separation between disciplines, circulated widely on both sides of the Atlantic and, as in the case of Geertz's *Thick Description*, credit the Institute's School of Social Science as the home base of an intriguing and appealing new perspective.

And finally, in those years numerous translations of Hirschman's works (monographs and collections of essays) came out in some European languages—a trend that correlates well with the extraordinarily large number of honorary degrees awarded to him around the world during that period (perhaps 18), which further increased the influence of his ideas.

It is also true, on the other hand, that this cultural offensive had important political implications. The Reagan presidency of the early 1980s represented the triumph of conservative cultural predominance in America. Social-political concerns related to this prompted the Ford Foundation to appeal to a group of "liberal" intellectuals, Hirschman included, about what to do. This was the origin, as mentioned above, of the research process that would eventually lead Albert to another masterpiece, *The Rhetoric* (1991). By that time, however, an important new event had attracted his attention—the fall of the Berlin Wall.

"Re-entry" strategies

(5) Thus, there are many ways. Some are the ones that Hirschman identified and practiced during the course of his long life. But there are undoubtedly others, many others (as our author would add at this point). In each of them, the important thing is never to lose sight of the goal to be achieved and to know how to properly perform one's chosen role, aiming for non-ephemeral results—current and future. Undoubtedly, Albert closely followed the complex and progressive genesis of the European Community, directly at first (during

economic analysis more generally, are beginning to be more widely questioned; the notable advances made by historians using social-scientific methods have led many social scientists to recognize that their own disciplines have been needlessly restricted by present-mindedness; and there has been a remarkable recrudescence of normative social and political philosophy. Yet positivist methodologies, with their allegiance (conscious or unconscious) to an empiricist set of assumptions about the theory of knowledge, still exercise the greatest influence on the profession in America."

the Marshall Plan), and then through intermediaries (mainly through his sister Ursula and brother-in-law Altiero Spinelli[311]).

But inevitably, his relations with different European countries had always been relatively uneven.

In short, it is safe to say that since his first exodus, France and Paris (his adopted city) had always played a privileged role in his cultural interests (and ventures). French had long been the language of the Hirschman household, part of his familiar lexicon. The special consideration Italy enjoyed from Albert (but not Sarah) was more private than public, because of Eugenio Colorni and what Albert called "the family" (sisters Ursula and Eva and numerous nieces and nephews); while Britain, for the most part, received respect and esteem. Finally, the Iberian world[312] was explored starting first with the former colonies—which did not, however, prevent Hirschman from receiving honorary degrees in Spanish and Portuguese lands.

Surprisingly, through all of this Germany long remained "a blind spot."

It was not until the 1970s that Albert began to have his work translated into German. He returned to Berlin with his sister only in 1974, for a brief private visit. Nothing more than that. This was probably because Hirschman had been convinced since the beginning of the Cold War that only the defeat of the USSR could reopen the game. He had argued this in private, putting him (for once) on a collision course with his sister Ursula, who, with her emotional temperament, had accused him of becoming a warmonger and conformist.[313]

Then again, from a different angle this shows that Albert had never considered the German affair "settled." And how could he?

Furthermore, while supporting the gradual construction of Europe (the one we know; the one that started with the six Western European countries), it is likely that in his heart, he considered its growth to be stunted. His enthusiasm (expressed, typically, in few words), in speaking to Nicoletta Stame and me about Europe's prospects after the fall of the Berlin Wall says a lot about what he had in mind for Europe's future.

(6) Hirschman's "re-entry" into Germany was encouraged by Claus and Sabine Offe, who had spent a year at the Institute at Princeton, and by Wolf and

311 Among other things, in the early 1960s, acting from America, Albert facilitated the founding of the Institute of International Affairs in Rome.

312 Leaving aside the early events, of course—the Spanish War and then the journey from Marseilles to Lisbon across the Pyrenees in order to emigrate to America.

313 Cf. Adelman (2013, p. 257).

Annette Lepenies, who had spent three there, had been invited to join the Institute, but then declined and returned to Berlin.[314]

In 1980 the Hirschmans visited the Offes in Bielefeld.

Out for a drive with them in the car, Albert's German "reminded Claus of his grandparents." It was a kind of "linguistic archaeology," recalled Offe. Hirschman's tongue had been frozen in time, fluent in the anachronisms of a bygone world. Offe also noted a shift. Unlike his English voice, which was notably reticent, often mumbling, the returnee was lyrical, enthusiastic, and talkative—as if a different language brought forth a different persona.[315]

Ten years later, as mentioned, Albert and Sarah decided to move to the Wissenschaftskolleg for the academic year 1990–1991. "At first glance," Wolf Lepenies commented,[316] "he did not seem emotionally overwhelmed by his return. Emotions, however, came back when the four of us [Sarah, Albert, Annette and Wolf] went to the opera. I will not forget the expression on Albert's face while he listened to *Fidelio*, Beethoven's masterpiece in which compassion plays a major role—and the yearning for freedom for which Albert himself had fought so bravely in so many places in his youth."

Hirschman thus inaugurated his German adventure, which in the end would prove decisive in elevating (and "adjusting") his *magnus opus* through self-subversion, and in further spreading his beneficial cultural influence in Germany, Europe, and beyond.

For the German edition of *Exit* (1974), Albert had written an ad hoc introduction in which he confessed to having become aware, after the book's publication in the United States, of the Berlin roots of his inspiration—an open wound long suppressed.[317] And it is indeed surprising that it was the exit-voice

314 Cf., above, n. 15 of the Preface. Wolf and Annette Lepenies, esteemed Berliners from the East who had been invited to move to Princeton by the School of Social Science of the Institute for Advanced Study to collaborate directly with Albert Hirschman and Clifford Geertz (see, above, n. 7 of the Preface), had for a variety of practical reasons . . . ended up declining the invitation. Albert's gratitude to this couple can be seen in his dedication of *A Propensity*, his "German" book, to them. Among Hirschman's work, it is the only dedication to people who are not (or were not) family members.

315 Adelman (2013, pp. 617 and 618).

316 Cf. V.v.Aa. (2013, p. 23).

317 "The book," he wrote, "is dominated by the concern that the defection of the most potentially influential protest advocates will keep them from opposing the decadence with the force that would otherwise be possible. This situation is in some ways reminiscent of the fate of the Jews who continued to live in Germany after 1939. Almost all of the strong young men, like me, fled the field soon after Hitler's seizure of power, leaving behind a severely weakened community. Of course, regardless of whether the choice was to stay or

interaction developed out of that "sense of guilt" which enabled him, 20 years later, to write the historical-conceptual essay on the fate of the GDR (discussed in ch. 1), thus completing the maximum extension of the public polarity of the two main politicizations of his life.

Not least because, clearly, his (certainly unanticipated) emotional state during his Berlin sojourn (the first since the advent of Nazism), was fortunately the polar opposite of that of his departure from Germany more than half a century earlier.[318] What he now understood and wrote in Berlin benefited from being closely attuned to the liberating historical events of the time. It was in fact a favorable climate, even exhilarating at times (although, as we shall see, not without its difficulties and setbacks), that accompanied Hirschman in the preparation of the "German" essays we are now considering.[319]

(7) There is, however, another path that connects exit-voice interaction to the life as lived, one which in a sense, balances and complements the previous

leave, the possibility of being heard was in those years practically nil. However, it could very well be that the book was born out of thoroughly repressed guilt, which, however absurd from a rational point of view, is ultimately undeniable. It seemed right to point out this consideration in the German edition. October 1972" (1974).

318 There is also, in this regard, an inverted correspondence between theoretical evolution and the perception of personal feelings. In the Preface to the German edition of *Exit* (cf. previous n. 317) the exit-voice opposition leads the author to discover his own guilt as the ultimate source of the book, whereas in the essay on the fate of the GDR, it is satisfaction with the way things have turned out that guides Albert toward finally clarifying the importance of the exit-voice alliance.

319 This suggests then—this is my hypothesis—that it was precisely his participation, however limited and indirect, in the events leading up to and following that famous year of '89 that helped Albert to "unblock" himself further, to reconsider his experience from a different point of view (no longer burdened by silences, repressions, or bitter ironies), to identify in the interpretation of the facts a high road for his "re-entry" into German cultural life—to conceive, finally, via self-subversion, a general re-setting of his approach (starting with some important analytical correctives already acquired). He was thus able to look more confidently to the future (including the famous "social science for our grandchildren"—cf. Hirschman, *Morality* (1980; now in 1981), and, below, sec. 7 of the present chapter—in which moral considerations are not repressed, but are systematically mixed with analytical reasoning). The late Hirschman papers are without doubt a big step forward in this direction. To be convinced of all this only requires rereading the beginning of the essay on the fate of the GDR—the one that begins with the memorable "the year 1989 was greeted with something of a yawn" (1995, p. 9). Because in its characteristic style, it neatly represents the manifestation of a mind that is finally liberated, in tune with itself.

one. In fact, along with the discovery and use of these oppositions, Hirschman developed a process of gradual acquisition. I am referring, first of all, to the historical-logical journey from the discovery of the narrow margin of tolerance for poor performance, through the concept of "latitude," to the exit-voice interaction.[320] And second, to the fact that after having clarified the ultimate, Berlin-based roots of *Exit* just recalled, Albert questioned the meaning of this "finding" in the well-known lecture that concludes *Essays in Trespassing*, "Morality and the Social Sciences: a Durable Tension."[321]

The mutual exclusion between heart and mind, typical of the social sciences, he argued, is deeply rooted in our culture. The economist's "trained incapacity" (Veblen) may be so strong as to prevent even a self-confession of the moral source of his or her research. Nevertheless, he adds, being an unconscious moralist is not necessarily a bad thing.[322] Indeed, reflecting on the success of *Exit* and on the "Preface" to the German edition just cited, he states: "it was probably fortunate that I was not aware of those deeper moral stirrings when I wrote the book; otherwise, the presentation of my argument might have been less general, less balanced [. . .] and less scientifically persuasive."[323]

But is it correct to conclude from this, as Albert had at first written, that "one perhaps peculiarly effective way for social scientists to bring moral concerns into their work is to do so unconsciously"? An interesting critical discussion with some friends developed on this point,[324] and Albert was convinced.

320 Meldolesi (1995, ch. 6).

321 This is the acceptance speech for the Frank Seidman Prize in Political Economy, Memphis (Tenn.), 1980, which initially stemmed from Albert's participation in the March 1980 Berkeley conference discussed above (see sec. 15 of ch. 3; and n. 319 of this chapter).

322 "For the origin of this viewpoint cf. Hirschman (1968a), where, referring to a book by Judith Tendler, he states that interdisciplinary work seems to become even better if it is done unconsciously. (It is likely, however, that by this Hirschman also intends to communicate a second message [. . .]—it is better to undertake to complicate economics than to advocate for it, and it is better to develop interdisciplinary moral analysis, etc. without thinking too much about it)" (Meldolesi, 1995, p. 228, n. 10).

323 Hirschman (1981, p. 305). "I always felt this conflict (this may surprise you)," Kenneth Arrow wrote to Albert (on January 12, 1981; box 1, folder 8), "but I tended to repress emotion in favor of the 'cool' head, though not without some considerable feeling of guilt. Your speech has given me some encouragement that it was in the long run the best way."

324 Such as Quentin Skinner, Heinrich Ehrmann, Dennis Thompson, Michael McPherson. Would it not be better, wrote McPherson, to invite economists "to open themselves to critical reflections on the moral commitments they already have?" Albert answered that he agreed with this formulation, not least because "it opens up an interesting line of inquiry" (cf. Adelman, 2013, pp. 572–573).

The result was that he rewrote the last page of his conference lecture. "Once one has gone through the historical account and associated reasoning of this essay," he wrote, "once we have become fully aware of our intellectual tradition with its deep split between head and heart and it is not always beneficial consequences, the first step toward healing that split has already been taken. Down the road, it is then possible to visualize a kind of social science that would be very different [. . .]: a moral-social science where moral considerations are not repressed or kept apart, but are systematically commingled with analytic argument [. . .]; where the transition from preaching to proving and back again is performed frequently and with ease; and where moral considerations need no longer be smuggled in surreptitiously, nor expressed unconsciously, but are displayed openly and disarmingly. Such would be, in part, my dream for a 'social science for our grandchildren.'"[325]

Analysis of European Integration

(8) What is clear from this is that both the "Preface" to the German edition of *Exit* and "Morality" are part of the process of scientific rethinking and gradual re-politicizing that characterized the Princeton period we have been discussing.

But for an understanding of this mosaic, one key piece is still missing. I am referring to "Three Uses of Political Economy in Analyzing European Integration," an essay from 1979 written during a research residency at the European University Institute in Florence.[326]

It is clear that the topic, for Albert, represented a sort of "return to the scene of the crime."[327] But 30 years after the Marshall Plan, the author's accumulated experience and scientific arsenal had evolved so much that, inevitably, the conclusions he reached were much more thoroughly worked out. What emerged was a compact, complex text that encapsulates in a few pages a significant part of Hirschman's work and which, for that very reason, comes across as somewhat enigmatic. We need to observe it close up and see if we can decode it (*pro domo nostra*, of course). It will be recalled that in "Approaches" Albert supported discrimination against American goods, making an economic argument in favor of European integration that included—clearly—a political motivation. Now, in the 1979 essay, discussing the first of "three uses" he

325 Hirschman (1981, pp. 305–306).

326 Hirschman (1979; now in 1981, ch. 12).

327 Cf., above, secs. 1–6, ch. 2.

examines—"the politics of trade creation and trade diversion"[328]—Hirschman argues that if European integration is analyzed from an economic point of view, the aim must be to achieve the highest possible trade creation and the lowest possible trade diversion. From a political standpoint, on the other hand, this relationship is reversed, because aiming for high trade diversion helps overcome resistance to integration (since producers find it advantageous to replace diverted trade), while proposing moderate trade creation policies dispels their fear of being quickly ousted by competition.

Now, if Albert had reconsidered the Marshall Plan debates he participated in[329] from the perspective of this framework, he would probably have concluded that it would help explain what actually happened.[330] That is, that it was American impatience (dictated ultimately by geopolitical factors) to speed up European integration that carried the day. And that in the specific case of the European Payments Union, it was indeed the acceptance of discrimination against U.S. goods, along with the prospect of gradually creating trade between the different countries, that made it possible to overcome political resistance—the Europeans included.

(9) We now come to the second "use"—"Spillovers and linkages: a parallel between political integration and economic development." Up to now, Albert explains, integration has been analyzed from an economic point of view, assuming "given, fixed resources." But one of the main purposes of the Union is not the more efficient allocation of existing resources, but rather "their growth, through economies of scale, more intensive communication, more confident entrepreneurship and the like."[331]

So, it is possible that "positive economic (growth-promoting) and positive political (union-strengthening) effects should go hand in hand." But it is only

328 The distinction comes from Viner (1950).

329 Which here are not even mentioned. In other words, this essay is still from the time when Hirschman publicly supported the famous "half-truth" about the origin of *The Strategy* recalled in ch. 2, n. 93.

330 Cf., above, sec. 4 of ch. 2.

331 Hirschman (1979, 1981, p. 272). The reference here is to Scitovsky (1958) and Streeten (1964). Here once again Albert avoids any reference to his previous work—whether from the Marshall Plan or later. He probably did not want to overload the text with self-references, "a practice," he once told me, "I don't like." Nevertheless, the critic cannot help but note that this key point of resource creation as an effect of integration was argued very forcefully by Hirschman in *Approaches* (1950) (cf., also, above, n. 330). Not to mention, of course, *The Strategy*.

a possibility. In order to begin exploring it, Hirschman proposes establishing a kind of conduit between economic evolution and political evolution as parallel processes. There is "a certain formal similarity between them which makes it tempting to 'borrow' or 'translate' from one to the other." In fact, "the pace and progress of both economic development and of integration depend on whether 'one thing leads to another' in the face of strong resistance from existing institutions, social and political structures, attitudes, values and so on."[332]

"The idea," Albert clarified, "that political science is able to illuminate the dynamics of integration is owed in good measure to the [originally] 1958 book by Ernst Haas, *The Uniting of Europe*, and to its guiding concept of 'spillover,'" which "essentially articulated what was the unspoken strategy—the 'thinkful wishing'—of such architects of European integration as Jean Monnet."[333]

"The leading idea here," Hirschman adds further on, "is that, once freedom of trade is irrevocably established among a group of countries, compelling pressures will arise toward uniform tax, social security, and eventually also monetary and general economic policies, presumably because otherwise the disparities and uncertainties under which national producers would have to operate, would be intolerable. It sounds like la *force des choses* and a quite reasonable prediction." But . . . it did not materialize.[334]

(10) "*Perhaps*," the author argues, "*it was then the vigorous growth of the Western European economies in the fifties and sixties that made the spillover dynamic so much less compelling than had been thought*"—in the sense that "in an environment of all-round growth, very few existing firms were or felt threatened and therefore were not particularly interested in further integration moves that would equalize the conditions of competition."[335]

332 Hirschman (1979, 1981, p. 273).

333 *Ibid.*, p. 267. Indeed (pp. 273–274), "the virtue and appeal of Haas's analysis was precisely that with his 'spillover' he had identified forces that would make for progress toward European unification through incremental steps, in spite of the obvious resistance from the powerfully entrenched interests of the national state system. Thus, he wrote: '. . . it is inconceivable that the liberalization not only of trade, but of the conditions governing trade can go on for long without "harmonization of general economic policies" spilling over into the fields of currency and credit, investment planning and business cycle control [. . .]. The spill-over may make a political community of Europe in fact even before the end of the transitional period.'"

334 *Ibid.*

335 *Ibid.*, p. 274; emphasis in the original.

At this point the essay turns to economic development and launches a surprising line of parallel reasoning between Haas's political analysis and Hirschman's economic analysis—conceptions that were not only proposed for different domains, but also for different realities: advanced in Haas's case, backward in Albert's.[336]

"Merely at the linguistic level," the author explains, "Haas's 'spillover' sounds rather like my '(forward and backward) linkage effects' and also has something in common with my characterization of development as a 'chain of disequlibria.' It may therefore be of some interest to pursue this surface similarity. Just as Haas, I was looking for a compelling dynamic that would unfold in spite of manifold and entrenched resistances. For that reason, I emphasized the need for stronger spurs than the placid generation and investment of capital along the lines of the then popular Harrod-Domar growth model. The strategy of unbalanced growth in general and the backward and forward linkages in particular [. . .] were seen as supplying such a more compelling and directive push."[337]

In any case, "both the spillover and the linkage dynamic were less reliable than had been thought originally. They worked nicely enough for a while; but just as the spillover dynamic failed the integration process in the mid-sixties, so there appeared at about the same time some evidence (and much talk) about a leveling off of the process of industrialization via import substitution. [. . .] It became clear in retrospect that there was some justification for distinguishing between an 'early and easy' stage of import-substituting industrialization and a more halting and difficult subsequent stage."[338]

The main conclusion is that "forces that are expected to subvert quietly and a bit deviously the existing order through economic pressures rather than

336 This demonstrates the double logic of Hirschman's discourse. On one hand the analytic results refer to a specific and carefully limited field of investigation. On the other however, once achieved, it sometimes happens that they can be reused elsewhere—*mutatis mutandis*, of course. "Although he [Hirschman] had been long engaged in analyzing underdevelopment," we read in Rodwin and Schön, eds. (1994, p. 314), "it became clear over time that many of his observations applied equally to societies in the so-called developed world."

337 *Ibid.*, p. 275. "The parallelism," Hirschman writes (p. 275) "goes further. For Haas's spillover to function, it was necessary that there first be some initial integration move [. . .]. Similarly, for the backward and forward linkage dynamic to get under way, some fairly important initial import-substituting industries must first be in place." Furthermore, the spillover first arises "fundamentally because of interest-group pressures for further integration moves," while the linkage dynamic was based on the idea that due to the scarcity of foreign exchange, investment in existing businesses is favored comparatively.

338 *Ibid.* Cf., above, ch. 2, n. 185.

change it in the course of an open political confrontation tend to labor for that very reason under a specific handicap. The absence of a strong ideology [in a positive sense, obviously] under whose banners they can mobilize support when difficulties appear."

Later, Hirschman would speak of the absence of a feeling of common culture in Europe—as in the statement to the press in 1995 that we have chosen as the epigraph for this book. So, the question was left (and unfortunately remains) unresolved. In the process of European integration, it is not possible to rely *sic et simpliciter* on either political spillovers or economic linkages.

(11) For his "third use of political economy," Albert presents, finally, "Some uses of exit-voice reasoning." Two are specific, "Capital mobility, reform, and integration," and "Regional imbalances and integration," while the third, "Integrative and disintegrative crises," is general.

Whether from one side or the other, we arrive here at processes of interaction between the economic (exit) and political (voice) modes of action that can give rise to alternately positive or negative outcomes within the integration process.

The exit or threatened exit of capital tends to repress voice. It represents a restraint against arbitrary taxation, but it also holds a kind of veto power over public-interest reform policies undesirable to capitalists. Once effective integration has been achieved, Hirschman argues, the exit-voice relation would be re-balanced, and the question of reforms, shifted to the community level, would be easier to resolve.[339]

But this, it seems to me, does not exempt us from specific exit-voice analyses concerning the reforms needed during the long phase of transition toward unity in which we still find ourselves; nor does it exempt us from the need to understand the related issues—between states, and within each of them.

Similarly, the integration process can increase tendencies toward economic polarization between states and within them, undesirable consequences which, however, can be fought with compensatory policies.[340] Moreover, the integration process can mitigate regional conflicts within states,[341] creating a

339 "The ability of capitalist states to undertake reforms," Albert states (*ibid.*, p. 278), "is enhanced by the formation of political-economic units that are large and inclusive enough to make the blocking of reforms through large-scale capital flight impractical."

340 About which it is clear that Hirschman had considerable illusions at the time (cf., in this regard, *ibid.*, p. 279)—a probable consequence of his decision not to go into the merits of political-administrative operations.

341 "A protracted history of conflict and subjection as well as linguistic, religious and cultural differences," Albert maintains (ivi, pp. 86–87), often lie behind problems of this sort,

new forum—the community—that in a sense enables the regeneration of their voice.[342] But even here, as we know from the way things played out, the outcome has not necessarily been unambiguous—there would be some arguments from Spain, Belgium, and even Italy.

Finally, processes of integration are not necessarily one way. They can move forward or backward with successive crises that can be formulated in terms of exit voice. A disintegrative crisis "leads the individual members (i.e. nation states) to go it alone," while the integrative crisis "impels members to look for some concerted action [. . .] from the common organization that is in the process of being built and that may well be strengthened as a result of the new task it is called upon to assume."[343]

"Moreover, the injection of exit-voice reasoning," Albert concludes, "has not pretended to produce fundamental new solutions to some major puzzles of integration. What then is the point of the exercise? Perhaps that it sensitizes us to certain situations which can be effectively reformulated in terms of exit and voice. Such reformulations will not leave things exactly as they were: occasionally they will make us see the forces at work as well as possible options and outcomes in a new light. And that is about as much, I have come to believe, as we can expect from social theory."

(12) It may well be!—is the inevitable comment. But it is also true that, for the reader, an exercise such as this one on some of the major conundrums of European integration ended up (again) seeming somewhat enigmatic.

This was mainly because it unfolded on an interpretive level and ground to a halt when faced with the need for policy, for actually doing something. Perhaps Albert did not feel totally involved (having written the essay before his

which "have multiplied and intensified in the post-World War II period because the European national states have lost their previous status as world powers, a position that had offered special opportunities for *all* the citizens of these states; more important perhaps, that status was simply awe-inspiring and deterred any idea of challenging national unity." An interesting subject, which may play a significant role in the process of integration.

342 Hirschman argues (*ibid.*, p. 281) that the union "can act as a concerned third party [in conflicts between a region and the state] or even as an ombudsman in relation to the grievances of disaffected regions." These suggestions were made in the press on behalf of embattled minorities in Corsica and Northern Ireland.

343 *Ibid.*, p. 283. In the international crisis that turned into a sovereign debt crisis in Europe, both of these contradictory drives were clearly at work. Arguably, the integrative aspect, though still weak, availed itself of the unintended consequences of the disintegrative aspect that preceded it—just as envisaged in the text (cf. *ibid.*).

full "re-entry" into European affairs). Perhaps, when confronted with a horizon as complex as the one delineated by his "three uses," he did not feel he needed to advance specific directions, or even to indicate an explicit way to seek them. Or even because, for precautionary reasons, he preferred to keep such a trajectory under wraps.

In fact, one need only reflect for a moment on Albert's "three uses" and the way they are set out in the text, one after the other—that is to say, in the way they actually developed on the ground (the inception, the initial success, and then the difficulties of European integration) and in the development of the Hirschmanian elaboration that is linked to it.

This small exercise is enough to show how, in relating them to a process such as European integration over an entire historical era, these "uses" should never be lost sight of. Indeed, they can be "revisited" as we go along—possibly proceeding in reverse, as if they were written in Arabic—as a means of deciphering the concrete situations we find ourselves in.

Often, exit and voice are opposed to one another, but as we now know better than before, they can also reinforce one another. Either way, we can look for interactions that set recovery processes in motion. Furthermore, once these processes have been launched, political spillovers and economic connections can be discussed (and pursued) in parallel, and the opposing political and economic yo-yo can be brought under control. And finally aspects of trade creation and trade diversion may have a role in the resulting picture.

The interest of the exercise then becomes one of keeping the entire palette in mind as we mentally apply ourselves to one or more of the problems of integration.

(13) To illustrate this, let us take an example. Suppose that a country is engaged in a gradual "entry" (or "re-entry") within EU constraints.

This does not mean that, at the same time, its government should not be thinking about reaching an understanding with European peoples and partners to positively advance the policies of the Euro-zone. And it immediately becomes clear that the better it is at resolving its own issues (by repairing public finances, solving regional crises, reversing the flow of capital in its favor, restarting development, etc.) based on the "three uses" and others as well, the more it will regain authority *urbi et orbi*, and the more it will have a voice, not least at the European level.

And vice versa: the more voice the better the solutions, perhaps triggering, through successive interactions, a potential virtuous circle.

Toward a New Approach

(14) If it is true, as Hirschman often declared (and the preceding pages show), that he had always worked for Europe's benefit, albeit in different ways from one phase to the next, it is also true that his extraordinary "revival of interest" in the 1980s and 1990s, at an advanced age, calls for particular scrutiny.

This was a period in which I knew and worked with him close up—to the point that I (sometimes) felt that I was part of the European project he was pursuing and which accelerated greatly after the fall of the Berlin Wall.

Nicoletta Stame and I had a clear sensation at the time that the job of disseminating Hirschman's work in different European countries was turning into an unexpected intellectual surge that was fundamentally supranational and "Berlin-based."[344]

Actually, the short text that Albert prepared for his honorary degree at the Berlin Freie Universität (1988),[345] he utilized "Opinionated opinions and Democracy"—a culmination of the intellectual "production line" that had started with *The Rhetoric*—as if to offer a final judgment (and democratic solution) regarding an intransigent past political culture that was now to be buried.

In addition, his presence at the Wissenschaftskolleg following the fall of the Wall led to a number of key German-language texts[346] which, as Albert wrote,[347] marked his re-entry into Germany's intellectual arena. Finally, I remember vividly how at some point in the early 1990s, Hirschman decided to accelerate the pursuit of an implicit project that we were unable to get him to spell out in detail—to the point that he reproached Nicoletta and me with, "How can you call yourselves Europeans if you are not at home in Berlin?"[348]

344 Berlin being the main center of activity and interest. (We got this idea from, among other things, Sarah Hirschman's decision to begin studying German . . .).

345 Along with some personal recollections: cf. Hirschman (1995, p. 77).

346 Of which the first ("Exit, Voice, and the Fate of the German Democratic Republic") was discussed above in ch. 1, and the last ("Melding the Public and the Private Sphere: Taking Commensality Seriously") in ch. 3. To them, two other essays should be added "Industrialization and Its Manifold Discontent: West, East and South"—see sec. 17 below—and the important "Social Conflicts as Pillars of Democratic Market Society." Finally, the Introduction to *A Propensity* and a large part of "Four Reencounters" originated in Berlin (cf. 1995, p. 2).

347 Cf., above, n. 15 of the Preface.

348 The practical consequence was that we actually purchased a studio apartment in Berlin as an instrument in a project (important but still unspecified) that first with Albert, then on our own behalf, we have always intended to follow through on.

I reflect on all of this in order to begin to capture (to the extent that I can) a still largely unexpressed idea that has been with me ever since. Indeed, there is no doubt that in retrospect, the campaign to publish Hirschman's works in France, Germany and Italy took hold as the European situation was moving toward the turning point of the fall of the Wall—and then the end of the Cold War, the vast realignment that followed (German reunification included), the enlargement of the European Community, etc. In a word, toward the archiving of an entire historical era and the unfolding of a new phase (which, however, is proving to be much more complex than expected).

And there is also no doubt that Albert's flurry of honorary degrees and other awards in so many European countries was part of the process that anticipated and accompanied that upheaval.

(15) But perhaps that is not all there is to it. The very issue of self-subversion is inevitably affected by the atmosphere of the time. It is as if Hirschman, once he had found the plot line and had set about re-examining his famous monographs one by one, had been seized by a desire to gradually *rebalance* his thinking in the light of the lessons received in the meantime from reality so as to make his work more useful in the new phase that had now begun, and to prepare himself to handle it in the best possible way.

Note, from this point of view, the beginning of the essay "A Propensity to Self-Subversion."[349] Citing the little story of the Jewish mother giving her son two ties for his birthday, Albert clarifies his way of working—criticizing the "compulsion to theorize as an obstacle to understanding," but always in search of theoretical concepts corresponding to the reality of things.[350]

It is precisely for this reason, he seems to be suggesting here, that he developed the idea of self-subversion, a reflex in the nature of "it ain't necessarily so" in "reaction to *one's own* generalizations or theoretical constructs."[351] This is followed in the essay by a number of self-subverting examples successfully brought into port, relating to *National Power*, *The Strategy*, *Exit*, and *The Rhetoric*.[352]

349 Hirschman (1995, ch. 5); originally written for the seminar on Hirschman's work organized by Lloyd Rodwin and Donald Schön, held at MIT (1992–1993).

350 Indirectly, if I am not mistaken, the "family debate" over "les belles lettres" resonates even here. Sarah often repeated that "literature is life," while for Albert (obviously) it was a source of inspiration.

351 Hirschman (1995, p. 87). Cf. ch. 1 above, sec. 11, and n. 82.

352 Why now, particularly? In my opinion the foreign translations, new forays and the beginnings of self-subversion had created the preconditions for such a turning point. That is to

"In closing," Albert writes,[353] "I should therefore like to [. . .] plead the virtue and attractions of indulging that activity. In the first place, I believe that what I have here called self-subversion can make a contribution to a more democratic culture in which citizens not only have the right to their individual opinions and convictions but, more important, are ready to question them in the light of new arguments and evidence. Furthermore, just as Gaston Bachelard said of Freudian repression that it is 'a normal activity, a useful activity, better still, a joyful activity,' so engaging in self-subversion can actually be a positive and enjoyable experience."

(16) Hirschman always felt that it was in the interests of America and Europe (not to mention Latin America, which he never forgot) to *learn* from each other.[354] So that as a result of the great change produced by the fall of the Berlin Wall, he most likely felt that, going forward, the democratic and social role of Europe could increase and the dialogue between the two sides of the Atlantic could improve the interrelationship between the two continents (and even between the three continents), to the great benefit of Western civilization and the life of the planet in general.

Moreover, Albert always believed in the need to support positive trends. In the United States, together with other intellectuals (often secular people of Jewish origin), he was part of an informal "liberal," democratic, pro-European current, taking initiatives that were sometimes intertwined with salient episodes in his life (such as that of the republication in 1993, with an introduction by Hirschman, and the new title *Assignment: Rescue*, of Varian Fry's book on the rescue of two thousand or more intellectuals and political refugees in Marseilles in 1940).

Actually, this liaison ended up having some limited but positive influence on the redefinition of German post-unification identity, and even contributed

say, it is also the political turn that suggests the intellectual one. And the fact that Albert criticizes the use of "*Wende*" (turn) to refer to the revolution that led to the fall of the Wall (*ibid.*, p. 42: cf. ch. 1 above, n. 85) speaks volumes (perhaps unwittingly) about the magnitude of the healing earthquake—objective certainly, but also subjective—in which he found himself.

353 *Ibid.*, pp. 91–92.

354 See, for example, what he wrote on this point in *Rival Views of Market Societies* (1986, p. 133), where, recalling Hartz's 1955 book, he affirms that America lacks what Europe has in spades—namely, a cultural differentiation that allows the organization of politics around two clear and well-defined poles.

indirectly to America's own evolution. I remember, for example, that when Albert arrived once in Berlin a journalist asked him what the Germans could do for the United States. Hirschman answered: "They can acknowledge their genocide—the Holocaust—in no uncertain terms, which will help the Americans recognize theirs"—of the Native Americans.[355]

Taking advantage of the opportunities offered by the many honorary degrees he received in that period, he made public many details of his actions before and during the war (through short texts, partly collected in the second part of A *Propensity*, which, as a counterpart to self-subversion, is devoted precisely to self-affirmation).[356]

Indeed, it is partly through tangible acts like these that so many ambiguous judgments about twentieth-century German history, common currency in the days of the Germany of Bonn, have now been overcome. One need only walk around Berlin to realize how important the memory of Hitler's persecution is today for defining the new identity of unified Germany.[357]

(17) Albert had arrived in Berlin without any pre-established program, intending to listen and learn. Along with other German, Hungarian, Polish, and Romanian scholars, he took part in a colloquium on the "Transition from Planning to the Market," and wrote an essay (originally in German, for the first time since 1932–1933)—"Industrialization and Its Manifold Discontents: West,

355 These developments also include the matter of the financing for the establishment of the Albert Hirschman Chair in Social Science at the Institute for Advanced Study in Princeton, New Jersey, in which, for the Italian portion, I participated together with Umberto Colombo and Tommaso Padoa-Schioppa. The decisive contribution came from the Deutsche Bank, which like so many other German private institutions, probably saw this as a good opportunity to signal a concrete change of course with respect to the past.

356 Also belonging to this trend is an autobiographical exercise of Albert's, *Passaggi di frontiera*, collected by Marta Petrusevitcz et al. and published in Italian in 1994. It later appeared in English translation in *Crossing* (1998): see, above, ch. 3, n. 211.

357 Indeed, signs of this new attitude are everywhere: in the Holocaust museums, in the brass plaques on the ground commemorating each persecuted person by name and surname in front of the building he or she lived in, in the small neighborhood museums in various city halls that reconstruct personal histories, in the bans against Jews in the 1930s attached to lampposts as imperishable reminders, etc. Cf., also, Lepenies (2006, p. 208). Faced with the many difficulties of the present, we must not lose sight of this positive aspect of today's Germany—a post-facto result (among others) of the uprisings of young people in the 1960s against their fathers, who had been Nazis. It is since then, Claus Offe told me, that the truth has really begun to take hold, *toto corde*.

East, and South"[358]—which, revisiting a typical issue of his from a new angle, "takes as its starting point two contrasting observations. One results from a look at the industrial establishment in Eastern Europe after the collapse of Communism, the other from my long-standing interest in Latin American economic development." "To a person conversant with Latin American development," he adds, "it is striking that the principal critique of industrialization in the East, that is, the priority given to heavy industry and the neglect of consumer goods, is the exact opposite, a mirror image in fact, of a critique of industrialization that is or has been widespread in Latin America." In conclusion, "East Europeans should perhaps become acquainted with the Latin American critiques, for in this manner they might realize that *their* industrialization was not wholly misguided."[359]

Afterwards, Albert became passionately involved with the path that led to "Exit, Voice, and the Fate of the German Democratic Republic." It can be said, then, that in the early 1990s, closely following this astonishing (intellectual, historical, political, cultural) exploit of Hirschman's, Nicoletta Stame and I took part, albeit indirectly, in a profound change that was taking hold in the heart of Europe and perhaps would produce consequences of great significance, even long time later.

(18) But at some point, the upward trend of the collective movement (sometimes overwhelming, as we could see for ourselves when we visited the Nicolaichirche in Leipzig) came to a halt and the enthusiasm waned. Albert, returning from an excursion to Eastern European countries, told us laconically, "It will take time"—a statement that froze our impatience in its tracks. He later explained to *Il Corriere della Sera*, in a sidebar to *il Mulino*'s pieces on the "fate" of the GDR, "the people in the East have their own cultural identity and their own mentality resulting from forty years of totalitarianism. And sometimes they miss the reassuring 'niches' of the old regime. They feel uncomfortable in capitalism, where you have to move in order to survive, and where the state does not offer a clear ideological message, does not indicate a direction of travel." And alluding to xenophobic tendencies, he added that "the scenario is very dark."[360]

358 "The title of this paper," Albert points out at the beginning of the essay (1995, p. 197), "obviously takes off from Freud's classic essay '*Das Unbehagen in der Kultur*' or 'Civilization and its Discontents.'"

359 *Ibid.*, pp. 198 and 210.

360 Hirschman, interview with *Il Corriere della Sera*, November 8, 1992. Box 75, folder 12.

Hirschman, therefore, decided to scale back his Berlin engagement. I thought he had opted, temporarily, for a more cautious course—perhaps in order to devise new developments later. Correspondence with Wolf Lepenies from that period shows, in fact, that he was continuing with preparations at the Wissenschaftskolleg for a long-planned "Colloque" with interested and knowledgeable people on his work.[361]

But another factor intervened—his health did not hold up. Albert had the fall in the mountains.[362] From that moment (as his sister Eva confirmed to me in Rome) "he was no longer himself." There was a long decline, which at a certain point turned into progressive agony. With *Crossing Boundaries* (1998) and his last illuminating essays (cf., above, Chapters 2 and 3), Hirschman had to grudgingly accept the human end of his extraordinary scientific season.[363]

361 Unlike the one in Bielefeld in 1988, which had been somewhat disappointing: cf. Box 5, folder 10 and 16. In the first folder there is even a list of scholars to be invited at the Berlin "Colloque," along with their fields of expertise (I appear as "economist, historian of economic thought").

362 Cf., above, ns. 16 of the Preface and 271 of ch. 3, along with the dramatic testimony of his son-in-law Alain Salomon on the 11th of July fall in Vv.Aa. (2013) and Adelman (2013, p. 644). Cf., finally, the letter Albert wrote to Lepenies on August 16 in which he stated that he felt depressed and did not want to return to Berlin the following year, adding: "I feel no longer comfortable participating in group discussion" (Box 5, folder 10).

363 This was also the period of his English translation of Ursula Hirschmann's autobiography, which had come out in Italian under the title *Noi senza patria* [We without a country]. It was an unsuccessful effort, partly because in translating it Albert had a tendency, where he disagreed with his sister . . . to edit the text.

BIBLIOGRAPHY[364]

AA.VV. (1977) *Self-Perception, Mutual Perception, and Historical Development. A Proposed Collaborative Program between the School of Historical Studies and the School of Social Science*, typescript, October 13. Box 77, folder 5.

AA.VV. (1987) *The New Palgrave, a Dictionary of Economic Theory and Doctrine*, London, Macmillan.

AA.VV. (2013) *A Bias for Hope. Commemorating the Life of Albert O. Hirschman*, Princeton University Press, Institute for Advanced Study, paper n. 50 of the School of Social Science for the Hirschman Memorial (March 24, 2013), April.

AA.VV. (2013a) *Germania al voto. Ritratto di una nazione*, Corriere della Sera, September 19.

Adelman, J. (2013). *Worldly Philosopher. The Odyssey of Albert O. Hirschman*. Princeton University Press.

Asso, F., & de Cecco, M. (1987). Introduzione. In A. O. Hirschman (Ed.), *Potenza Nazionale e commercio estero: gli anni Trenta, l'Italia e la ricostruzione*. il Mulino.

Bell, D. (1983) *The American Academy of Arts and Sciences*, typescript. March 14.

Bissell, R. (1996). *Reflections of a cold warrior*. Yale University Press.

[364] All the texts with the indication "box, folder" come from the Albert O. Hirschman Papers (MC 160), Seeley G. Mudd Manuscript Library, Princeton University, Princeton, NJ. However, letters and interviews from this source have not been included in this bibliography to avoid overloading it.

Brubacker, R. (1991). Frontier theses: Exit, voice, and loyalty in East Germany. *Migration World, 18*(3–4).

Cardoso, F.H. (1996). "Preface" to the Portuguese edition of Hirschman, A. O. (1995). *A Propensity to Self-Subversion*. Harvard University Press.

Casanova, J. C. (1990). *Éloge du Professeur Albert Hirschman*, Doctorats Honoris Causa. Insitut d'études politiques.

Colorni, E. (1944). Prefazione. In A. Spinelli & E. Rossi (Eds.), *Problemi della Federazione Europea (Il Manifesto di Ventotene)*. English tr. E. Colorni, *Critical thinking in action. Excerpts from political writings and correspondence I* (L. Meldolesi & N. Stame, Eds., pp. 99–105). Bordighera Press.

Colorni, E. (1998). *Il coraggio dell'innocenza* (L. Meldolesi, Ed.). La città del sole.

Colorni, E. (2009). *La malattia della metafisica. Scritti filosofici e autobiografici* (G. Cerchiai, Ed.). Einaudi.

Colorni, E. (2016). *Microfondamenta* (L. Meldolesi, Ed.). Rubbettino.

Colorni, E. (2019). *Critical thinking in action. Excerpts from political writings and correspondence I* (L. Meldolesi & N. Stame, Eds.). Bordighera Press.

Colorni, E. (2019a). *The discovery of the possible. Excerpts from political writings and correspondence II* (L. Meldolesi & N. Stame, Eds.). Bordighera Press.

Colorni, E. (2021). *The Final Year: 1943–44. Genesis of a Perspective* (L. Meldolesi, Ed.). Bordighera, Press.

Colorni, E. (2021a). *"The philosophical illness" and other writings* (L. Meldolesi, Ed.). Bordighera, Press.

Colorni, E. (2022). *Art, Aesthetics, politics* (L. Meldolesi & M. Quaranta, Eds.). Bordighera Press.

Colorni, E., & Spinelli, A. (2020). *Dialogues* (L. Meldolesi, Ed.). Bordighera Press.

Coser, L.A. (1984). *Refugee scholars in America: Their impact and their experiences*. Yale University Press.

Crozier, M. (1986) *État moderne, état modeste*. Fayard.

Foxley, A., McPherson, M.S., & O'Donnell, G. (Eds.). (1986). *Development, democracy, and the art of trespassing. Essays in honor of Albert. O. Hirschman*. Notre Dame University Press.

Frobert, L., & Ferraton, C. (2003) *L'enquete inachevée: Introduction a l'économie politique d'Albert Hirschman*. Presses Universitaires.

Fry, V. (1945) *Surrender on demand*. Random; new ed., *Assignment rescue*. Scholastic, 1992.

Gehler, M. (2013) *Le Tre Germanie. Germania Est, Germania Ovest, e Repubblica di Berlino*, Odoya.

Gershenkron, A. (1952). Economic backwardness in historical perspective. In B. Hoselitz (Ed.), *The progress of underdeveloped areas*. Chicago University Press.

Gershenkron, A. (1962). *Economic Backwardness in Historical Perspective*. Harvard University Press.

Gershwin, G., & Du Bose, H. (1935). *Porgy and Bess*—opera; YouTube performance 2002.

Ginzburg, A. (2012). Sviluppo trainato dalla produttività o dalle connessioni: due diverse prospettive di analisi e di intervento pubblico nella realtà economica italiana. *Economia e lavoro, 2*.

Ginzburg, A. (2013) "Introduzione," "Dialogo. Crisi del debito o crisi dell'Europa?," *Economia e lavoro, 1.*

Haas, E. (1975). *The uniting of Europe* (Research series, No. 25). Institute of International Studies. University of California Press.

Heilbroner, R. (1953). *The Worldly Philosophers*. Simon.

Heinze, C., & Pollack, D. (1990). Zur Funktion der politich alternativen Gruppen in Prozess des gesellschaftlichen Umbruchs in der DDR. In W.-J. Gabner et al. (Eds.), *Leipzig in October.* Wichern.

Hidalgo, C.A., & Hausmann, R. (2008). *A network view of economic development*.http://www.ricardohausmann.com/doc_admin/upload/HidalgoHausmann_ DAI_2008.pdf2.

Hirschman, A.O. (1945). *National power and the structure of foreign trade* (3rd ed.). University of California Press, with a new Introduction, 1980.

Hirschman, A.O. (1947) "Exchange Control in Italy," Review of Foreign Developments, March 11 and May 6; tr. It. in Albert O. Hirschman, *Potenza Nazionale*, cit. 1987.

Hirschman, A.O. (1947a) "France and Italy: Patterns of Reconstruction," Federal Reserve Bulletin, n. 4; tr. It. in Albert O. Hirschman, *Potenza Nazionale*, cit. 1987.

Hirschman, A.O. (1947b) "Italian Exchange Rate Policy," Review of Foreign Developments, December 16, tr. It. in Albert O. Hirschman, *Potenza Nazionale*, cit. 1987.

Hirschman, A.O. (1948) "Inflation and Deflation in Italy," American Economic Review, September, tr. It. in Albert O. Hirschman, *Potenza Nazionale*, cit. 1987.

Hirschman, A.O. (1948a) "Economic and Financial Conditions in Italy," Review of Foreign Developments, December 14; tr. It. in Albert O. Hirschman, *Potenza Nazionale*, cit. 1987.

Hirschman, A.O. (1948b). Disinflation, discrimination, and the dollar shortage. *American Economic Review*, December; now in A. O. Hirschman. (2022). *Three continents. Political economy and development in Europe, the United States and Latin America* (L. Meldolesi, Ed.). Peter Lang.

Hirschman, A.O. (1949). *Proposal for a European Monetary Authority* (typescript); now in A. O. Hirschman. (2022). *Three continents. Political economy and development in Europe, the United States and Latin America* (L. Meldolesi, Ed.). Peter Lang.

Hirschman, A.O. (1950). *Approaches to Multilateralism and European Integration* (typescript); now in A. O. Hirschman. (2022). *Three continents. Political economy and development in Europe, the United States and Latin America* (L. Meldolesi, Ed.). Peter Lang.

Hirschman, A.O. (1951). Industrial Nations and Industrialization of Underdeveloped Countries. *Economia Internazionale*, August.

Hirschman, A.O. (1952). Effect of industrialization on the markets of industrial countries. In B. Hoselitz (Ed.), *The progress of underdeveloped areas*. Chicago University Press.

Hirschman, A.O. (1954). *Research project, case studies of instances of successful economic development in Colombia* (typescript, Box 36, folder 4).

Hirschman, A.O. (1954a). *Economics and investment planning: Reflections based on experience in Colombia* (typescript); now in A. O. Hirschman. (1971). *A bias for hope. Essays on development and Latin America.* Yale University Press.

Hirschman, A.O. (1956). *The market for paper and pulp in Colombia* (2 Vols., typescript).

Hirschman, A.O. (1957). Economic policies in underdeveloped countries. *Economic Development and Cultural Change*, July; now in A. O. Hirschman. (1971). *A bias for hope. Essays on development and Latin America.* Yale University Press.

Hirschman, A.O. (1958). *The strategy of economic development.* Yale University Press.

Hirschman, A.O. (1963). *Journeys toward progress. Studies of economic policy-making in Latin America.* Twentieth Century Fund.

Hirschman, A.O. (1964) "The Paternity of an Index," American Economic Review, September, now in A.O. Hirschman (1980) *National Power.*

Hirschman, A.O. (1967). *Development projects observed.* Brookings Institute.

Hirschman, A.O. (1968). The political economy of import-substituting industrialization in Latin America. *Quarterly Journal of Economics*, February; now in A. O. Hirschman. (1971). *A bias for hope. Essays on development and Latin America.* Yale University Press.

Hirschman, A.O. (1968a). Foreword. In J. Tendler (Ed.), *Electric power in Brazil.* Harvard University Press.

Hirschman, A.O. (1970). *Exit, voice, and loyalty: Responses to decline in firm, organizations and states.* Harvard University Press; German tr. *Abwanderungund Widerspruch.* Mohar, 1974.

Hirschman, A.O. (1971). *A bias for hope. Essays on development and Latin America.* Yale University Press.

Hirschman, A.O. (1977). *The passions and the interests. Political arguments for capitalism before its triumph.* Princeton University Press.

Hirschman, A.O. (1977a). A generalized linkage approach to development, with special reference to staples; now in A. O. Hirschman. (1981). *Essays in trespassing: Economics to politics and beyond.* Cambridge University Press.

Hirschman, A.O. (1978). Beyond asymmetry: Critical notes on myself as a young man and some other old friends. *International Organization*, winter; now in A. O. Hirschman. (1981). *Essays in trespassing: Economics to politics and beyond.* Cambridge University Press.

Hirschman, A.O. (1979). *Three uses of political economy in analyzing European integration* (typescript); now in A. O. Hirschman. (1981). *Essays in trespassing: Economics to politics and beyond.* Cambridge University Press.

Hirschman, A.O. (1979a). *Private and public happiness: Pursuits and disappointments* (typescript, Box 78, folder 1).

Hirschman, A.O. (1980). *Morality and the social sciences: A durable tension* (Acceptance Paper). P.K. Seidman Foundation; now in A. O. Hirschman. (1981). *Essays in trespassing: Economics to politics and beyond.* Cambridge University Press.

Hirschman, A.O. (1981). *Essays in trespassing: Economics to politics and beyond.* Cambridge University Press.

Hirschman, A.O. (1981a). The rise and decline of development economics. In A. O. Hirschman (Ed.), *Essays in trespassing: Economics to politics and beyond.* Cambridge University Press.

Hirschman, A.O. (1982). *Shifting Involvements. Private Interest and Public Action.* Princeton University Press.

Hirschman, A.O. (1982a) "Rival Interpretations of Market Societies: Civilizing, Destructive or Feeble?," Journal of Economic Literature, December, now in A.O. Hirschman (1986). *Rival Views of market societies and other recent essays.* Viking.

Hirschman, A.O. (1983) *Ascesa e declino dell'economia dello sviluppo ed altri saggi*, ed. A. Ginzburg, Rosenberg.

Hirschman, A.O. (1984). A dissenter's confession: Revisiting *The Strategy of Economic Development*. In G. M. Meier & D. Seers (Eds.), *Pioneers in Development*. Oxford University Press; now in A. O. Hirschman. (1986). *Rival views*.

Hirschman, A.O. (1984a). *Getting ahead collectively: Grassroots experiences in Latin America*. Pergamon.

Hirschman, A.O. (1984b). Against parsimony: Three easy ways of complicating some categories of economic discourse. *American Economic Review*, May; now in A. O. Hirschman. (1986). *Rival views of market societies and other recent essays*. Viking.

Hirschman, A.O. (1986). *Rival views of market societies and other recent essays*. Viking.

Hirschman, A.O. (1986a). Exit and voice. An expanding sphere of influence. In A. O. Hirschman (Ed.), *Rival views of market societies and other recent essays*. Viking.

Hirschman, A.O. (1986b). Linkages in economic development. In A. O. Hirschman (Ed.), *Rival views of market societies and other recent essays*. Viking.

Hirschman, A.O. (1987). *Potenza nazionale e commercio estero. Gli anni Trenta, l'Italia e la ricostruzione* (P. F. Asso & M. De Cecco, Eds.). Il Mulino.

Hirschman, A.O. (1987a). *Acceptance speech* for Honoris Causa degree in Political Science at the Università di Torino (November 12); now in A. O. Hirschman. (2022). *Three continents. Political economy and development in Europe, the United States and Latin America* (L. Meldolesi, Ed.). Peter Lang.

Hirschman, A.O. (1987b). *L'economia politica come scienza morale e sociale*, with an essay and edited by Luca Meldolesi. Liguori.

Hirschman, A.O. (1988). *Berlin Festvortag* (typescript); now in A. O. Hirschman. (1995). *A propensity to self-subversion* (ch. 7). Harvard University Press.

Hirschman, A.O. (1988a). *Come complicare l'economia* (L. Meldolesi, Ed.). Il Mulino; English tr. Cit. 2020.

Hirschman, A.O. (1989). Having opinions: One of the elements of well-being? *American Economic Review. Papers and Proceedings*, 2, May; now in A. O. Hirschman. (1995). *A propensity to self-subversion*. Harvard University Press.

Hirschman, A.O. (1990). *Tre Continenti. Economia politica e sviluppo della democrazia in Europa, Stati Uniti e America Latina* (L. Meldolesi, Ed.). Einaudi. English tr. A. O. Hirschman. (2022). *Three continents. Political economy and development in Europe, the United States and Latin America* (L. Meldolesi, Ed.). Peter Lang.

Hirschman, A.O. (1990a). Albert O. Hirschman. In AA.VV. *Economics and sociology* (R. Swedberg, Ed.). Princeton University Press.

Hirschman, A.O. (1990b). *Come far passare le riforme* (L. Meldolesi, Ed.). Il Mulino; English tr. Cit. 2021.

Hirschman, A.O. (1991). *The rhetoric of reaction. Perversity, futility, jeopardy*. Harvard University Press.

Hirschman, A.O. (1992). Industrialization and its manifold discontent: West, East and South. *World Development*, 20; now in A. O. Hirschman. (1995). *A propensity to self-subversion*. Harvard University Press.

Hirschman, A.O. (1993). Exit, voice, and the fate of the German Democratic Republic. *World Politics, 45*; now in A. O. Hirschman. (1995). *A propensity to self-subversion*. Harvard University Press.

Hirschman, A.O. (1993a). The rhetoric of reaction—Two years later. *Government and Opposition, 28*; now in A. O. Hirschman. (1995). *A propensity to self-subversion*. Harvard University Press.

Hirschman, A.O. (1993b). *Petit Discours de Nanterre* (typescript).

Hirschman, A.O. (1993c). *Coimbra Talk* (typescript); now in A. O. Hirschman. (1995). *A propensity to self-subversion* (ch. 10). Harvard University Press.

Hirschman, A.O. (1994). The on and off connection between political and economic progress. *American Economic Review. Papers and Proceedings, 84*; now in A. O. Hirschman. (1995). *A propensity to self-subversion*. Harvard University Press.

Hirschman, A.O. (1994a). Social conflicts as pillars of democratic market society. *Political Theory, 22*; now in A. O. Hirschman. (1995). *A propensity to self-subversion*. Harvard University Press.

Hirschman, A. O. (1994b). *Passaggi di frontiera*. Donzelli.

Hirschman, A. O. (1995). *A propensity to self-subversion*. Harvard University Press.

Hirschman, A. O. (1996). *Melding the public and the private sphere: Taking commensality seriously*. Jan Patochka Memorial Lecture. Institute for Human Sciences; now in A. O. Hirschman. (1998). *Crossing boundaries. Selected writings*. Zone.

Hirschman, A.O. (1997, June). *Fifty years after the Marshall Plan: Two posthumous memoirs and some personal recollections* [Conference]. Harvard University; now in A. O. Hirschman. (1998). *Crossing boundaries. Selected writings*. Zone.

Hirschman, A.O. (1998). *Crossing boundaries. Selected writings*. Zone.

Hirschman, A.O. (2020). *How economics should be complicated* (L. Meldolesi, Ed.). Peter Lang.

Hirschman, A.O. (2021). *How reforms should be passed* (L. Meldolesi, Ed.). Peter Lang.

Hirschman, A.O. (2022). *Three continents. Political economy and development in Europe, the United States and Latin America* (L. Meldolesi, Ed.). Peter Lang.

Hirschman, A.O. (2023). *The postwar economic order. National reconstruction and international cooperation* (M. Alacevich & P. F. Asso, Eds.). Columbia University Press.

Hirschman, A.O. and Lindblom, C. (1962) *Economic development, research and development, policy making: Some converging views*, Rand Corporation, April.

Krali, A. (2012) *Primi della Klasse. La crisi europea e il ruolo della Germania*, Cairo.

Lepenies, W. (2006). *The seduction of culture in German history*. Princeton University Press.

Mann, H. (1918). *Der Untertan*. Wolff.

Marjolin, R. (1986). *Le travail d'une vie*. Laffont.

Marshall, T.H. (1949). *Citizenship and social class*. Alfred Marshall Lectures. Cambridge University; now in Marshall, T.H. (1965). *Class, citizenship and social development*. Doubleday.

Meier, G.M., & Seers, D. (Eds.). (1984). *Pioneers in development*. Oxford University Press.

Meldolesi, L. (1985). Gli spiriti del capitalismo. Alcune osservazioni a partire da Hirschman e Braudel. *Stato e mercato, 15*.

Meldolesi, L. (1985a). America, America. Note su Hirschman, Hartz e Braudel. *Inchiesta, 69*, July–September.

Meldolesi, L. (1987). Alle origini del possibilismo: Albert Hirschman 1932–52. In A. O. Hirschman. *L'economia politica come scienza morale e sociale*, with an essay and edited by Luca Meldolesi. Liguori; French tr. *Revue française de science politique*, *3*, 1993.

Meldolesi, L. (1987a). Economia e politica vent'anni dopo: mutevoli coinvolgimenti e fruttuose convergenze. *Inchiesta*, *78*.

Meldolesi, L. (1987b). Per una nuova ipotesi interpretativa della storia del pensiero economico moderno. *Quaderni di storia dell'economia politica*, *1–2*.

Meldolesi, L. (1988) "Introduction," to A.O. Hirschman *Come complicare l'economia* (L. Meldolesi, Ed.). Il Mulino; English tr. Cit. 2020.

Meldolesi, L. (Ed.). (1990). "Introduction," to A.O. *Hirschman: Tre Continenti*. Giulio Einaudi.

Meldolesi, L. (1990a) "Il futuro ha un cuore antico?," *Economia politica*, *2*.

Meldolesi, L. (1990b) "Introduction," to *Come far passare le riforme* (L. Meldolesi, Ed.). Il Mulino; English tr. Cit. 2021.

Meldolesi, L. (1990c) "Mezzogiorno, con gioia," *Nord e Sud*, *2*.

Meldolesi, L. (1991–92). Gli spiriti del capitalismo. *Modernizzazione e sviluppo*, *1–2* and *3*.

Meldolesi, L. (1992). *Spendere meglio è possibile*. il Mulino.

Meldolesi, L. (1992a). Braudel e un "Post-scriptum." *Il Ponte*, *10*.

Meldolesi, L. (1994). *Alla scoperta del possibile. Il mondo sorprendente di Albert O. Hirschman*. il Mulino; English tr. University of Notre Dame Press, 1995; Spanish tr. Fondo de Cultura Econòmica, 1997.

Meldolesi, L. (1994a). Sulla nozione di squilibrio ottimo. In G. Caravale (Ed.), *Equilibrio e teoria economica*. il Mulino.

Meldolesi, L. (1994b). Problemas de reforma do Estado: crime, corrupção, trapaça, parasitismo, incùria. Sucessos, limites e lições do caso italiano. *Revista Brasileira de Ciências Sociais*, *24*.

Meldolesi, L. (1995). *Discovering the possible. The surprising world of Albert O. Hirschman*. University of Notre Dame Press.

Meldolesi, L. (1996) *Il giuoco degli dèi. Un'angolazione di politica economica*, Rubbettino.

Meldolesi, L. (1998). Introduzione. Colorni per tutti. In E. Colorni (Ed.), *Il coraggio dell'innocenza* (L. Meldolesi, Ed.). La città del sole.

Meldolesi, L. (1998a) *Dalla parte del Sud*, Laterza.

Meldolesi, L. (2000) *Occupazione ed emersione*, Carocci.

Meldolesi, L. (2001) *Sud: Liberare lo Sviluppo*, Carocci.

Meldolesi, L. (2004) *Emersione. Dialogo con Marco Biagi*, Carocci.

Meldolesi, L. (2007) *La quarta libertà. Come padroneggiare la pubblica amministrazione*, Bonanno.

Meldolesi, L. (2009) *Il nuovo arriva dal Sud. Una political economica per il federalismo*, Marsilio.

Meldolesi, L. (2010). *Federalismo democratico. Per un dialogo tra uguali*. Rubbettino.

Meldolesi, L. (2010a). *Milano-Napoli. Prove di dialogo federalista*. Guida.

Meldolesi, L. (2011). *Italia federanda*. Rubbettino.

Meldolesi, L. (2012). *Federalismo possible. Per liberare lo Stato dallo statalismo e i cittadini dall'oppressione*. ESD.

Meldolesi, L. (2013). *Imparare ad imparare. Saggi di incontro e di passione all'origine di una possible metamorfosi*. Rubbettino.

Meldolesi, L. (2013a), *Carlo Cattaneo e lo spirito italiano*. Rubbettino.

Meldolesi, L. (2014). *L'ultimo Hirschman e l'Europa. Esercizi teorici sull' "auto-sovversone."* Rubbettino.

Meldolesi, L. (2017). *Albert Hirschman, entre Europe y América Latina. Reflecciones teóretico-práticas desde una perspectiva colorniano-hirschmaniana.* Universidad National de Quilmes, .

Monnet, J. (1976). *Mémoires.* Fayard; English tr. Doubleday, 1978.

Murray, O. (1982). Symposiumund Mannerbund. In P. Oliva (Ed.), *Concilium Eirene*, xvi.

O'Donnell, G. (1986). On the fruitful convergences of Hirschman's *Exit, Voice, and Loyalty* and *Shifting Involvements*: Reflections from the recent Argentine experience. In A. Foxley, M.S. McPherson & G. O'Donnell (Eds.), *Development, democracy, and the art of trespassing. Essays in honor of Albert. O. Hirschman.* Notre Dame University Press.

Offe, C. (1990). *Wohlstand, Nation, Republic: Aspekte des deutschen Sonderweges von Sozialismus zum Kapitalismus* (typescript).

Ostrom, E. (1990). *Governing the commons.* Cambridge University Press.

Pollack, D. (1990a). Religion und gesellschaftlicher Wandel. *Ubergange*, June.

Pollack, D. (1990b). Das Ende einer Organisationsgesellschaft. *Zeitschrift fur Soziologie*, August.

Ritter, H. (1989). Abwandern, Widersprechen: Zur aktuellen Bedeutung einer Theorie von A.O. Hirschman. *Frankfurter Allgemeine Zeitung.*

Rabinow, P., & Sullivan, W.M. (Eds.). (1979). *Interpretive social science: A reader.* University of California Press.

Rodwin, L., & Schön, D.A. (Eds.). (1994). *Rethinking the development experience: Essays provoked by the work of Albert Hirschman.* Brookings Institution.

Rossi, E., & Spinelli, A. (1944). *Problemi della Federazione Europea (Il Manifesto di Ventotene)* (E. Colorni, Ed.).

Rossi-Doria, M. (2011). *Una vita per il Sud. Dialoghi epistolari 1944–1987* (E. Bernardi, Ed.). Donzelli.

Rostow, W.W. (1960). *Stages of economic growth.* Cambridge University Press.

Samuelson, P.A. (1954). The pure theory of public expenditure. *Review of Economics and Statistics, 36.*

Samuelson, P.A. (1955). Diagrammatic exposition of a theory of public expenditure. *Review of Economics and Statistics, 37.*

Schmitt Pantel, P. (1992), *La Cité au banquet: Histoire des repas publics dans les cites grecques.* Ecole Française de Rome.

School of Social Science. (1977). *Self-perception, mutual perception, and historical development. A proposed collaborative program between the School of Historical Studies and the School of the Social Science* (typescript, October 13. Box 77, folder 5).

School of Social Science. (1977a). *Our view of social science* (typescript, Box 4, folder 12).

Scitovsky, V.T. (1958). *Economic theory and Western European integration.* Allen.

Scitovsky, V.T. (1976). *The joyless economy: An inquiry into human satisfaction and consumer dissatisfaction.* Oxford University Press.

Scott, R.J. (1986). Dismantling repressive systems: The abolition of slavery in Cuba as a case study. In A. Foxley, M.S. McPherson, & G. O'Donnell (Eds.), *Development, democracy, and the art of trespassing. Essays in honor of Albert. O. Hirschman.* Notre Dame University Press.

Simmel, G. (1910). Die Soziologie der Mahlzeit; now in G. Simmel. (1984). *Das Individuum und die Freiheit: Essais*. Wagenbach.

Spinelli, A., & Rossi, E. (1944). *Problemi della Federazione Europea (Il Manifesto di Ventotene)* (E. Colorni, Ed.).

Stame, N. (1996) "Avaliçao das polìticas pùblicas na França," *Revista do service public, 1*.

Streeten, P. (1964). *Economic integration*. Sytoff.

Symons, M. (1994). Simmel's gastronomic sociology: An overlooked essay. *Food and Foodways, 4*.

Tendler, J. (1968). *Electric power in Brazil*. Harvard University Press.

Tietel, S. (Ed.) (1992) *Towards a New Development Strategy for Latin America: Pathways from Hirschman's Thought*, Inter-American Development Bank.

Times Literary Supplement. (1995, October 6). The hundred most influential books since the war.

Torpey, J. (1991, June). *Exit, voice, and loyalty in the "Peaceful Revolution" in the GDR* (typescript). University of New Hampshire.

Vianello, F. (2013). La moneta unica europea. *Economia e lavoro, 1*.

Viner, J. (1950). *The customs union issue*. Carnegie Endowment.

Vitale, M. (2008). *Viaggio nell'economia campana. Presentazione sintetica*. Guida.

Vitale, M. (Ed.). (2013). *Linee programmatiche per Umberto Ambrosoli. Sintesi delle conclusioni del gruppo di lavoro n. 1 su: economia, sviluppo, lavoro, imprese, programmazione, territorio* (typescript).

Whitehead, A. N. (1930). *Process and reality*. Macmillan.

Zapf, W. (1991). *Der Zusammenbruch einer Sozialstruktur* (typescript).

INDEX OF NAMES

www.ingramcontent.com/pod-product-compliance
Ingram Content Group UK Ltd.
Pitfield, Milton Keynes, MK11 3LW, UK
UKHW020842290926
15470UKWH00004B/1501

9 781636 675404